Medicine Men of
Hooper Bay

CHARLES E. GILLHAM

Medicine Men of Hooper Bay

More Tales from the Clapping Mountains of Alaska

ILLUSTRATED BY CHANIMUN

THE MACMILLAN COMPANY, NEW YORK
COLLIER-MACMILLAN LIMITED, LONDON

To my children
Edward Lehne
and
Lucia Lee

The Macmillan Company, New York
Collier-Macmillan Canada, Ltd., Toronto, Ontario
Library of Congress catalog card number: 66–10283
Printed in the United States of America
First Printing

Contents

Introduction

For centuries the Eskimos lived alone on the Bering Sea in Alaska, cut off from the outside world by ice, mountains, and snow. Only recently have traders, churches, and schools come to them with the civilization of the white man.

They had no doctors to care for their ills and injuries. They had no church to guide them. Instead they had Medicine Men, or Shamans, who, they believed, were all-powerful. These men were supposed to perform miracles of healing. The fresh skin of a rabbit might be applied as a poultice to an infection. Our doctors tell us that this is very bad. An acute stomachache might be treated with dancing and songs held in the Kashim, the meetinghouse of the Eskimos.

Food is all-important to the Eskimos. They must have fish, seals, or birds or they starve. Often the Medicine Men would hold ceremonies to bring more fish and seals close to the shore. Their religion was closely tied to Nature. They believed they were descended from the Crow Man. The sea held mysterious goblins who sometimes caused men and kayaks to disappear. Conversations might be carried on between a Medicine Man and animals. The great ones could walk under the sea and not get wet. They could be consumed by fire and appear again unharmed. Since they are Oriental in origin, it is small wonder that some of the mysticism of the East came with them.

An old Eskimo who had been trained to become a Medicine Man, before the churches and schools appeared to discourage him, is the source of the following folk stories of these interesting people. He acted out many of his tales, and his eyes burned with excitement as he related them.

It is most difficult to persuade the Eskimos to tell their stories. Many of the younger generation have never heard them. The old ones have forgotten them, or they feel that these tales are something the white man has no business to know. Eskimos are a bashful people. The older ones, knowing little of the English language, are embarrassed when they try to tell the stories handed down to them throughout countless generations. Without a written language—and Eskimos have none—how many of the pioneer stories of our land would we know? It would be the task of a lifetime to try to gather even a few of them.

Along the coast of the Bering, Eskimo hunters traveled from village to village in ancient times. They usually stopped as long as they were welcome, staying in the Kashim, or Man House, as it is sometimes called. Their price of admission was usually a good story. No doubt many of their yarns were based on imagination only. With the retelling, they gathered color as other hunters ventured farther along the coast to visit neighbors.

Some of the earlier travelers in Alaska have related some of the same stories I heard at Hooper Bay many years later. Dr. E. W. Nelson, of the U.S. Biological Survey, briefly recorded a few in his notes more than sixty years ago. Schoolteachers in the Indian Service have attempted to gather Eskimo folk stories. Few of them have ever been published.

Hooper Bay is south of Norton Sound and Nome. Because of the shallow waters guarding it from the sea, few boats put into the village. I spent two summers with the Eskimos of this region. One year I went to the village by dogsled. Starvation was just around the corner. Each day we drove our poor dogs out to the sea hoping for a chance shot at a seal or a goose. Living with these people, who were cheerful and hopeful of better hunting on the morrow, I began to know something about them. I found that seals, eider ducks, and emperor geese were more important to them than anything else on earth.

Huddled behind our shooting blind of ice cakes,

while the ice pack ground and roared just offshore, I marveled at the endurance of these people. Blue with cold, they stuck to their business of hunting. Little ones in the igloos must be fed. I stayed with them. I would have felt guilty not to, for food was badly needed in the village. Maybe because I hunted with the Eskimos they regarded me as different from the few other whites they had previously met. At any rate, they told me their stories. I pass them on to you.

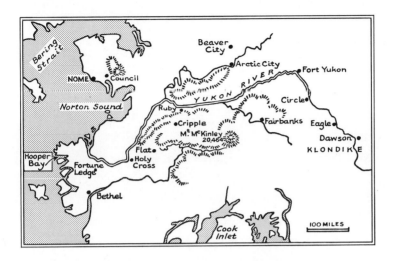

Neshmuk the Miracle Man

ONE of the greatest of all the Medicine Men of Hooper Bay was Neshmuk. He lived so long ago that many of the famous things he did have been forgotten. Not only was he a great man with fire, as was Pynaytok, who later followed him, but he could change the weather, as did Nayatok, another great Shaman. He did many things to show the people how strong his power was.

Once he asked the Eskimos to gather a huge pile of dry wood. When they had done this he climbed on top of it and told them to set fire to it. He was dressed in the clothes he always wore. He had on a muskrat-skin parka and trousers of drill. Over his muskrat parka he wore five seal-gut rain parkas. On his feet were fine boots made of spotted sealskin. Around the tops of them was the fur of the ermine. In his hand he held a magic wand. On one end of the wand were tied beautiful feathers from the cormorant and the eagle. On the other end was an ivory point, or pick, which the Medicine Man used to test the ice.

Soon the pile of wood was a raging mass of flames. The Medicine Man sat on top of it without feeling any pain. As the wood burned, so did the Medicine Man. When the fire went out, there was nothing left but fine white ashes. All the people returned to the village. They gathered in the Kashim to discuss what they had seen. Suddenly they heard a sound from the porch. In walked the Medicine Man. He had no burns. He was wearing the muskrat parka and the five seal-gut parkas and his trousers of drill. They were not burned. His spotted sealskin boots were as they were before. Not even one hair of the fine ermine fur was as much as singed. The feathers on his wand were not at all scorched. The people realized that Neshmuk was a very powerful Medicine Man with very strong medicine.

Often Neshmuk would change the weather. If the wind was blowing the wrong way for the hunters, he would go out on a hill, throw his knife into the air, and sing. Often he would catch the knife by the handle. Or he might step quickly aside and the falling knife would stick into the ground. Then the wind and weather would usually change. Sometimes it did not change right away. Like all weather, even in Alaska, it would be different after a while. Then the Eskimos would say how powerful Neshmuk was.

In the Asunuk Mountains is a large rock the Eskimo people call the Whale Rock because it looks exactly like a whale. They think the Crow Man left it there many years ago when he first made the mountains. Probably he did. Often Neshmuk would run into the side of the large rock and go right through it. There would not even be a hole where he went through.

He could stick the feathers of birds upright in the hardest of rocks or upon slabs of wood. They would stay there, standing on end, in the strongest of winds. If anyone else tried to do such a thing, the feathers would break or fall over and blow away.

This great Miracle Man, Neshmuk, could lift the water just as the Crow Man could. Often he put on his muskrat parka and five seal-gut parkas and walked beneath the water. One time he came to a giant seal net set under the ice of the Bering Sea. It was so long that he could not walk around it and so deep that it went from the bottom of the ocean clear to the top. He tried to make a hole in it to get through, but it was so strong that he could not. Then he dived into it like a fish and tried to wriggle through the meshes. They were so strong that he was unable to do so. He returned to the village, warning the Eskimo people never to put a net around the point from Hooper Bay again. Something with a giant net was using that place. No seals could be caught there, anyway, because the net filled the whole ocean.

Then the Eskimo people set their nets around in the bay in front of the village. They never did set them out in the ocean any more. Sometimes the Medicine Man would see whether the big net was still there. It always was. When he went to look at the net, the Eskimos would always take their nets out of the water so that he would not get into any of them by mistake. Once a man forgot to take out his net when Neshmuk walked upon the bottom of the ocean. For two days Neshmuk did not return. Then one night he came into the Kashim dripping wet. The man's net was wrapped tightly around his body.

When the people saw this they knew for sure that Neshmuk had been walking on the bottom of the ocean. The net was so tightly wrapped around him that no one could take it off. Then the man who had put out the net tried to remove it. The minute he touched the

4

net it fell clear of Neshmuk to the floor of the Kashim. That proved that it belonged to the man who had forgotten to take it out of the ocean when Neshmuk walked beneath the water.

The Medicine Man would sometimes perform tricks in the Kashim just to show how powerful his medicine really was. He would have someone tie his feet tightly together and then tie his hands behind his back. Next a rope would be tied from his neck to his feet and around a wooden post in the floor of the Kashim. The light would be covered with a large blubber pot and the whole Kashim would be dark. In a few seconds the pot would be removed and the Kashim would be light again. Neshmuk would be sitting in the same place. All the ropes would be in a pile at his feet and he would be free.

In the roof of the Kashim a heavy cord hung down from the ceiling. Just beside it was an iron ring. Sometimes when the people were in the big room, the Miracle Man would point to the string hanging down from the ceiling. He would ask someone to cover the light for an instant and then uncover it again. When this was done he would point to the heavy string. It would not be hanging down any more but would be through the hole in the iron ring. Then if the light was covered again for a few seconds the Medicine Man would say some magic words, and when the light was uncovered the string would be hanging down and not be through the iron ring.

Thus Neshmuk was the most powerful Medicine Man who ever came to Hooper Bay. One day he left to walk the bottom of the ocean. He never returned. The people were very sad. Some think he got into the big net and could not free himself. Others think he was captured by the Old Man of the Sea. At any rate, he did not return. What do you think happened to him?

"Never Sleepy Man"

For a long time after Neshmuk disappeared under the sea, they had no Medicine Man at Hooper Bay. At last the "Never Sleepy Man" came. He was called the "Never Sleepy Man" because he was always telling the men in the Kashim not to sleep so much but to get out and do things. The Kashim was such a sleepy place that his preachings did very little good. Someone was always telling a story, and the Eskimo men did spend too much time in there sleeping.

The "Never Sleepy Man" did not have the powers of Neshmuk, but he was a good man and cured the sick. He spent much of his time looking around in the ocean to see just where the seals and the fish were. Often he brought them close to Hooper Bay and made it easy for the people to get them. He could walk under the water like Neshmuk, but he usually swam like a seal.

One spring there were few seals, and the "Never Sleepy Man" set out to find them. In the night he went into the water and set off beneath the waves. When morning came he was far to the South, near Nunivak Island. As he swam past the village of the beautiful harbor, he suddenly popped his head up, far offshore, in the channel. In the Kashim at Nunivak were two very powerful and wicked Medicine Men. Although they sat there with their eyes closed and appeared to be sleeping, they saw the "Never Sleepy Man" in their medicine as he popped up out in the channel of the ocean.

"We must kill this powerful Medicine Man who swims so far from his home," they told each other. "He will take all our seals and our fish. There will be none here for us."

They called several of the Eskimo men and said they must help to catch the "Never Sleepy Man."

"He is sure to come back this way," said the Medicine Men, "so we will change the channel from out in the beautiful harbor to make it flow right through the porch of our Kashim." They said magic words and actually changed the channel that went from Nunivak to Tununa. The water now flowed through the porch of the Kashim.

"Now," they told the Eskimo men, "weave some mats of grass and place the mats over the porch of the Kashim so that they touch the water. When the 'Never Sleepy Man' swims through the channel, he will come right through this porch. His head will touch the mats of grass and raise them, showing us that he is here."

Then the Medicine Men made two great harpoons, much larger than those used in hunting seals, and they handed them to the best harpooners in the village.

"When you see the grass mats lift, the 'Never Sleepy Man' will be at the porch of the Kashim. Then you must strike as hard as you can with the harpoons. We must kill him."

The "Never Sleepy Man" traveled far in his search for the seals. When he found them he saw that they were going toward Hooper Bay. That was well.

He then started back the same way he had come, past Nunivak Island and the beautiful harbor. He did not know that the wicked Medicine Men were trying to kill him. Neither did he know that the channel had been changed. On he swam, straight up the channel and under the porch of the Kashim.

Suddenly his head struck the grass mats. He knew something was wrong. He dived as deep as he could, with all his strength. But the harpooners had seen the mats move. They threw the terrible spears as hard as they could through the mats of grass and hit the "Never

Sleepy Man" in the back. Pulling as hard as possible, he broke the thongs that held the harpoons. With both of them buried deep in his back, he returned to Hooper Bay.

He did not tell the people he had the terrible harpoons in his back for fear they would lose faith in him and his medicine. Instead he told them the seals were coming and began making a dancing mask.

"I am making this mask for you because I will not live," he told them. "Always wear this mask in the spring to make the seals come."

As the winter came to an end, the "Never Sleepy Man" grew very thin. He ate nothing but snow.

"When the snow is gone I shall die," he told the people at Hooper Bay. "But always keep the mask I made. Then you will have plenty of seals in the spring."

The bad Medicine Men on Nunivak Island were watching in their medicine as the "Never Sleepy Man" became thinner. They knew he could never get well. One night they made very powerful medicine. It caused the two harpoons to return to them under the sea.

So when the last of the snow disappeared from the tundra behind Hooper Bay, the "Never Sleepy Man" died. He was buried on a little hill where he could look out toward the sea and watch for the seals. The people at Hooper Bay did not know that the wicked Medicine

Men at Nunivak Island had caused his death. If they had known, they would very likely have started a war with the people there. The "Never Sleepy Man" knew this. That was why he did not tell anyone about the harpoons in his back. He did not want fighting, for he knew that such a thing is very wrong.

The Hooper Bay people kept the mask, and every spring they used it in their dances, which are part of a ceremony asking the seals to return. They always remembered the "Never Sleepy Man."

Even today when some man spends too much time in the Kashim telling stories or sleeping, his wife will say to him, "You had better remember what the 'Never Sleepy Man' said. Go out and hunt something for us to eat."

We should remember, as do the Eskimo people, that it is not good to be sleepy all the time and never to do our work.

Chanimun

Pynaytok the Fire Man

PYNAYTOK was one of the old-time Medicine Men at Hooper Bay. He lived long before the white men came to Alaska. His son was Nayatok, who found the villages in the sky and brought mild weather and fish to the people of the village. In many ways, however, Pynaytok did even greater miracles than any of the other Medicine Men.

Once there lived a man who had never been able to walk. From the day he was born he had lacked the use of his legs. When he was of age he crawled to the Medicine Man and pleaded, "Oh, Pynaytok, can you help me? Please cure my legs so that I may walk like other people. I cannot hunt and I cannot fish. If I do not have legs, I will starve when a hungry year comes."

"I will try to help you," Pynaytok said, "so that you can hunt." He asked the people to gather a great pile of driftwood and burn him and the crippled man together. The wood was piled upon the edge of the ice, for this was in the springtime. The Medicine Man and the poor crippled fellow climbed upon the pile.

"Now, set the driftwood alight," the Medicine Man told the people, "and return to your Kashim and play the drums. I am going with this man to see if he can be cured so that he may walk." The wood was set on fire, and the people left.

Soon the blaze was roaring about the Medicine Man and the crippled fellow. However, neither of them felt the heat. They were perfectly cool. As the smoke grew very thick, the crippled man fainted or fell asleep—he did not know which.

When he awakened, the crippled man was lying on the sand beneath the ocean. He looked around. He was all by himself. To the north he could see black ice that looked as if it had been burned. "That," he said to himself, "is where I was when Pynaytok and I were burned."

He looked to the south and saw clear icebergs beneath the water. There were tracks on the bottom of the ocean leading around them.

The man got to his feet and took a step. He could walk! His legs did not hurt. Quickly he followed the tracks of the Medicine Man. When he went through the channel around Point Dall he entered the bay, and in a few minutes the tracks led out of the water. The man found himself in front of the Kashim in the village. He went inside and the drums were still playing. When the people saw him walking, the drums stopped beating.

Pynaytok spoke to him. "Now you can walk as well as any man. Because you were cured, you must do something to pay for it. You must not marry for one year." The man agreed to this.

Before the year was out, the crippled man broke his promise. He felt so well and could hunt and fish so easily that just the day before the year was up he married a pretty girl in the village. At once he became a little lame. He knew he had done wrong. Although he could still walk and hunt, it always hurt him a bit and reminded him that one must never break a promise.

Once Pynaytok went to Point Dall with an Eskimo man to get the wood to make a frame for a skin boat. Together they worked at shaping the light, strong driftwood sticks to make the ribs and the gunwales of the boat.

When they had finished, the man said, "Now we will have to carry these sticks home. It will be a very heavy load for us."

"No," Pynaytok answered him, "we will not have to carry the sticks. I will take them back to Hooper Bay by my medicine."

Then he directed the man to break all the sticks for the boat into kindling wood. Soon there was a large heap of kindling on the ground. Then Pynaytok climbed upon the broken sticks and said to the man, "Set this alight and I will burn with it. As soon as you have lighted this wood, run to Hooper Bay village as fast as you can."

The man was very frightened, but he did as he was told. As soon as the fire started, he ran swiftly toward the village. When he was about halfway there, he heard something whiz past him through the air. He could see nothing but a white streak. On he ran as fast as he could.

When the man reached the village, he saw the people swimming in the little lake in front of the Kashim. He ran to them and quickly told them what had happened. But as he came to the bank of the lake, he stopped short and stared. He could not believe his eyes. There in the water with the other people was Pynaytok the Medicine Man. By the side of the lake, he saw the pieces of the skin boat that he had broken up. But they were no longer broken. They were all together and ready to be covered with mukluk skins.

All who heard this agreed that Pynaytok was indeed a great Medicine Man. He continued to work miracles until he died, when he was a very old man. He told the people that when he died they must cut off his head and boil it in a big pot. This they did by heating rocks in the fireplace and dropping them into the water in the pot.

Then they took the body of the great Medicine Man and buried it so that his head was under the fire pit. Today the Kashim people always speak of Pynaytok the Fire Man and of how he did not wish to be buried like the other Medicine Men up on the hill. Even after his death, he always wanted to be close to the fire.

How Nayatok
Brought Warm Weather

At Hooper Bay in Alaska, on the Bering Sea coast, the Eskimo people have had some great Medicine Men. One of the greatest was Nayatok, the son of Pynaytok, one of the most powerful Medicine Men ever known.

Nayatok was especially noted for his skill as a Weather Man. He performed many feats to bring rain, to change the direction of the wind, or to bring mild weather. Often he would go out on the hills behind

Hooper Bay and make medicine, throwing his knife into the air as he chanted his songs. Quite often the direction of the wind would change.

Once when the Eskimo people had had no rain for months, Nayatok went into the tundra alone and made such powerful medicine that he lifted a lake up into the sky. For days afterward it rained so hard that the people were afraid it might never stop. In fact, it rained so much that the lake he put in the sky filled up again. You would never have known that the Medicine Man had used it in the first place.

During one of the hungry winters, the people at Hooper Bay were very distressed. It had been cold for so long, with a north wind, that the ocean froze over solid. It is very bad when this happens, for then there are no seals to be had along the edge of the ice. Soon people are without food. Then a hungry year comes. Unless the weather can be made warmer, many people will starve.

Nayatok saw that something had to be done quickly if the people of Hooper Bay were to be saved from starvation. If he changed the wind to a south wind it would take too long for the thick ocean ice to melt. So although it was midwinter and extremely cold, the only way to save them would be to bring warm weather with rains. Ice quickly breaks up when warm rains fall on it.

In the Kashim, the Medicine Man told the people that he would make the most powerful medicine he could. He took two loon eggs and placed them gently in the middle of the skin of a large yellow-billed loon. Then he sat on them himself to hatch them out. He did not do this as the birds do, by sitting quietly on the eggs for a long time. Instead he handed a drum of walrus skin to a little Eskimo boy and said, "Play it, my son, and never stop until I tell you. There is a very powerful medicine to be made. Beat ever so carefully, my son, and I shall sing."

Then Nayatok began to chant:

> *Come from your eggs, weather birds;*
> *Hatch out, baby loons;*
> *Break from the shell, with your sharp beaks,*
> *While I sing other tunes.*

The little boy drummed on. It was very still in the Man House. How everyone hoped that the medicine would be strong and the little loons would hatch out! Finally Nayatok got up from his nest on the loon skin, took another drum, and began to dance and sing. The little boy danced, too. Suddenly the Medicine Man pointed to the loon eggs in the nest. They were beginning to open up. From within, the tiny birds were pecking as hard as they could at the shell to get out.

Then the shells fell apart and two little loons stood up. They were brothers.

Nayatok continued playing his drum and dancing. Then he sang another verse to his song:

> *Hurry loons and grow large,*
> *That you may fly away*
> *And bring us rains and warm sunshine,*
> *That spring may come to stay.*

Faster and faster the Medicine Man danced and beat on his drum. Faster and faster the little Eskimo boy played on his drum, too, keeping time with Nayatok. As the people watched, the tiny loons grew. At first they had only fine silky down on their little bodies. It looked like fur. Then it grew coarser; and on their tiny wings, little feathers began to appear. Soon the loons were twice as large as they had been when they came out of the eggs. As they went on growing, Nayatok sang another stanza of his song:

> *Grow faster yet, oh little birds,*
> *And soon big loons you'll be;*
> *To bring mild weather, ere we starve,*
> *Make haste to melt the sea.*

Nayatok was now beating his drum so fast that the little Eskimo boy could hardly keep up with him. His back and arm ached terribly, but he did the very best he could. Surely he was helping to make great medicine. Before the eyes of the people in the Kashim, the loons kept getting bigger. Soon there were feathers all over them. They seemed to swell like balloons. Then suddenly the Medicine Man stopped his song and laid his drum upon the floor of the Kashim. The little Eskimo boy stopped playing his drum and placed it beside the one Nayatok had been using.

Everyone turned and looked again at the brother loons. They stretched their necks and slowly spread out their wings and tried them. Then, with a bow to the Medicine Man, they sprang lightly into the air and flew straight out through the porch of the Kashim.

Everything was very quiet. No one talked. It was the most powerful medicine any of them had ever seen. The light in the seal-oil lamp burned low. An old woman was bending over it to trim the wick. Suddenly she straightened up and listened. All of the other people listened, too. From the south they clearly heard the roll of thunder. On the walrus-stomach window in the top of the Kashim, they heard the patter of rain.

Then everyone shouted with joy. They knew that the terrible hungry year was over. A hunter stepped out of the Kashim and quickly returned to say that a warm south wind was blowing. From the ocean they could hear the ice moving. Soon there would be seals and blubber for everyone.

That is how Nayatok brought warm weather, and even today the Eskimo people always watch the loons to see what they are doing. They think that the loons are weather prophets. They can tell by the way the loons call when there will be rain and mild weather. In the autumn the loon always tells people, by its calls, when the cold weather is coming.

It is rather silly, isn't it, when some people say "as crazy as a loon"?

The Villages in the Sky

ONCE upon a time, long before the white men came to Hooper Bay, the people were without fish. There had been a hungry winter. It was the year when Nayatok the Medicine Man had worked a miracle by hatching two loons and sending them out to hunt for mild weather. Spring had come at once, and with it the seals. But the fish, which usually came right after the seals, had failed to appear. This was a great blow to the people, who needed the fish badly. Nayatok decided that he would see whether he could get fish for the Eskimo people.

One night in the Kashim, the Medicine Man called

23

for two of the best drummers in the village. They were Chieftoolgak and Uyureukarak. Both were young men and very strong. They could drum for more than a day without stopping. Nayatok handed each a walrus-skin drum and told him to settle himself comfortably. He was about to take a long journey, and they would have to play for all that time. Then he put on a muskrat parka and five seal-gut parkas over that. Taking his two medicine wands, he departed into the night. On one of the wands was a flounder, a small flat fish; on the other was a whale.

Walking to the edge of Hooper Bay River, Nayatok lifted up the water and stepped beneath it. He then closed the water down over him and walked on the river bottom. He was looking for the tracks of a great Medicine Man who had often brought many fish to Hooper Bay. This great man had walked the bottom of the ocean many times, until one time he failed to return. Nayatok thought that he might get help from this great man in bringing the fish to the Eskimo people, if he could only find him.

No sooner had Nayatok entered the water than he found the tracks of the great one. They were leading up along the bottom of Hooper Bay River and not toward the ocean at all. They were leading straight toward the mountains. It was not easy to follow the tracks, for they were quite old. Finally, at a bend in the stream many miles from Hooper Bay, the tracks left the river and turned up the bank. Nayatok followed them. Then they came to an end on the land. Nayatok looked up and saw that they rose into the sky.

Following in the same tracks made by the great one, Nayatok climbed, higher and higher, until he could not see the earth below. Soon he passed the clouds. It was rather dark, and the tracks were hard to see. Onward he went until at last he came out into a beautiful land in the sky. Right in front of him was a large lake. On the banks of the lake was a village.

Nayatok walked around the edge of the lake and passed by the village without stopping. In the center of the town, near the Man House, he saw a pole. At the top of it hung a red fox-skin parka. He saw no people; but from the fur parka he knew that this was the land where lived the Eskimo people who had frozen to death on earth. He passed the village of the frozen people and followed the edge of the lake. Soon he came to another village.

In the center of this one was a Man House, and by it stood a pole. Hanging from this was a water pail of clay. When Nayatok saw the pail, he knew that this was the village of the people who had died of thirst on the earth below. He saw no one, so he went on around the shore of the big lake. Soon he came to another village.

A food basket made of woven grass hung on top of a pole near the Man House. Nayatok knew that this was the village of the people who had starved to death on the earth below. Because he saw no one, he walked on around this village and soon came to another.

Before the Man House in the center of this village was a pole. At the top of this was a sharp arrow. Nayatok knew that this was the village of the people who had been killed in wars on the earth below. He hurried on past it, for he saw no one.

After walking quite far, Nayatok came to a river that flowed out from the lake. In the center of this river were three sandbars. As he drew nearer, he saw that they were not sandbars but the skins of three huge fish. In the middle of the river sat a man in a kayak, fishing. His little boat was low in the water. It was almost filled with fish. Looking more closely, Nayatok saw that it was the great one, the man who had always brought plenty of fish to the people of Hooper Bay.

He called to him, "Oh, Great One, show me how to find fish for the people at Hooper Bay. They are very hungry, and soon they will starve."

The great one looked up at Nayatok and replied, "Cross this river on the white rocks you see below here. If you fall in, do not be afraid, but do as you think best."

Nayatok went to the rocks in the river. The current was very swift. He stepped on the first rock and started across to the second rock. The next one was white and round and just under the water. The Medicine Man stepped on that one and it rolled out from under his feet. Splash! In he fell, into the swift river, and was swept down with the current.

Soon he came to a fish trap built across the stream. He hit it with such force that he made a hole in the willows of which it was built and went rushing on. Then he passed through another fish trap, and another, and another. Dead ahead in the river he saw two icebergs. One was little, and the other was a big one covered with the white hair of baby spotted seals. He swam to the little iceberg and climbed on it. He did not go to the big one, for he knew that if he did there would always be ice in Hooper Bay.

No sooner had Nayatok climbed on the little iceberg than it quickly sank. He found himself on the bottom of the ocean, where many different kinds of fish swam around. Before him under the water he saw an igloo. He walked to the door and knocked. A man opened the door. There was a woman inside. Both wore parkas of fishskin. Nayatok saw that these people had fins on the back of their parkas and on their heads. The fins were moving.

The woman looked at the Medicine Man. "What do you want here?" she asked.

"I came for fish," Nayatok replied. "The people at Hooper Bay are starving. I wish to bring fish to my people."

The woman reached under her bed and pulled out part of a dried king salmon. "Here, take this," she said. "It will bring plenty of fish to your people." She moved her fins back and forth as Nayatok took the salmon and put it into the pocket of his parka. The man opened the door, and the Medicine Man set out for Hooper Bay, walking under the water.

Soon he reached the channel at Point Dall. The water was so thick with fish that their sides rubbed his shoulders as he pushed his way between them. As he drew near to the village, the fish were so plentiful that the Medicine Man had to get out on the bank and walk.

Inside the Kashim, the two drummers were still singing and playing on the walrus-skin drums when Nayatok walked in. He was very wet from his trip beneath the sea. The drummers were very tired, for they had played all night. Walking to the middle of the Man House, the Medicine Man raised his hand. The drums stopped.

Then he spoke. "The bay is full of fish," he said. "You may catch as many as you want. A woman at the bottom of the ocean gave me a piece of dried salmon. It has brought the fish to the people. I have hidden this good omen well. Whenever we need more fish, I shall use it again."

Sure enough, the next day the men brought fish to Hooper Bay in kayak loads. There were salmon, herring, whitefish, and flounder. With the fish came the young mukluk seals, or loftak, as the Eskimo people call them. Everyone was happy. People had as many fish as they could eat. As long as Nayatok lived, there were always plenty of fish because he had safely hidden away the piece of dried salmon that the woman had given him.

Many years later, after Nayatok's death, there came again a time when the people of Hooper Bay could catch no fish.

"Does anyone know where the Medicine Man left that piece of dried salmon?" the people asked one another. "If we could only find it, we could have fish and not starve."

Nayatok had a son whose name was the same as his father's. He, too, was a Medicine Man. But as he was rather young, his medicine was not as strong as that of his father.

"I will try to find the dried salmon," he told the people. "Then we may have good luck again with our fishing." So he played the walrus drum in the Kashim and sang songs and looked deep into his medicine. Finally he arose. He left the Kashim and went to a small river west of Hooper Bay. Looking carefully into the water, he saw a very large clam. It was the biggest he had ever seen.

Young Nayatok took the clam out of the water and opened it. Inside this clam was another. He opened this and found still another. This he did five times. The last clam was not very large. When he opened it, there was the piece of dried salmon the woman at the bottom of the ocean had given his father many years ago.

Young Nayatok hurried back to the village and told the people that he must have a man and a woman to help him. He took a small medicine drum from the wall. He gave the man a medicine stick with a flounder on it and the woman a medicine stick with a whale on it, and he led them to the little river west of Hooper Bay.

He placed the little drum in the exact middle of the stream. "Now," he said to the woman, "spear the little drum with your medicine stick and pin it down into the mud." The woman did this.

"Now," he said to the man, "spear the drum with your medicine stick and pin it down into the mud also." The man did as young Nayatok told him.

"Look through the two holes you have made in the little drum," young Nayatok said to the man and woman. "You will see the piece of dried salmon which was given to my father many years ago by the woman under the ocean." They both looked and saw the good omen inside the drum under the water.

"Now," said young Nayatok, "you have seen the good omen, and you know I have found it. We have hidden it again in the little drum. Should anything ever happen to me, you will know where it is. It will never be lost again."

Ever since that time, the people of Hooper Bay have had good fishing, for the good omen has never been lost. Even today, about a mile from the village, you can see the grave of Nayatok on a little hill. Standing straight up in the ground are his two medicine wands, one with a little flounder on it and another with a whale.

A man should never keep his secrets entirely to himself. He should tell them to his children, for someday they might need to know them.

Niyak and the Eagles

Iɴ an Eskimo village on the Bering Sea coast of Alaska, there once lived an orphan boy named Niyak. His father had been taken by the Old Man of the Sea as he hunted seals far out on the ocean; his mother had died when Niyak was very small. He could remember neither of them. He lived in the village with his old grandmother. She was a very wise old woman. She knew about as much as most of the Medicine Men.

Like all orphans, Niyak was different from other little boys. He could see and hear things they could

32

not, and he knew even more than the grown men. His name meant "Seal" in the Eskimo language. Niyak was a very well-behaved little boy.

In this same village lived an Eskimo girl named Umuk. Her father was the very best hunter in all the Eskimo land. She was a very beautiful girl, and she liked the little orphan boy very much. Often she would invite Niyak to go out with her to gather berries or to hunt for birds' eggs in the springtime. She even told him he could wear her father's water boots and his fine kuspuk, or hunting coat. The orphan boy did not go with her until one autumn day. All the children were going out of the village to gather grass, so he decided to go along.

It is very important for the Eskimos to gather grass. They use it for many things. When all the children go, it is like a picnic or a game to pull up the long straight grass and place it in bundles. Sometimes the grass is used in the igloos to sleep on. It is always used in the funny short boots the Eskimos wear to keep their feet warm when they walk on the snow. Little Umuk wove some of her grass into baskets. All the men of the village had fine grass mats in the bottoms of their kayaks to keep the little boats dry. Grass is certainly a very useful thing to the Eskimo people.

When all the children started back to the village with their bunches of grass, Niyak called to Umuk. She was on the other side of a hill. He said they must be going, for all the other children had already started.

"In a minute," she called back. "I have just a little more grass to get to make my bundle large enough. I will come in just a minute."

Niyak lay on his back on the hillside, looking into the sky and watching the birds. He saw a long-tailed jaeger, a graceful, pretty bird. He smiled because it was named Umuk, too, the same as the little girl. He could hear her busily pulling grass only a short distance away. After a while he did not hear her any more and went to look for her. She was gone. Quickly Niyak walked around the little hill. He could see all over the whole country from the top of the little hill. Umuk was nowhere to be seen. It seemed as if the earth had swallowed her up.

All afternoon the little orphan called and looked for Umuk. As night came he returned to the village without her. He went to her father, the great hunter, and told him what had happened. With two of the best Medicine Men in the village, the father went to the hill to look for his daughter. They searched all night.

The hunter could find the tracks where Umuk had walked around picking grass. He was very good at trailing animals and could see where anything had walked. But now he came to the place where his daughter's tracks ended. The Medicine Men looked up into the sky and told the hunter they could see her tracks leading straight up into the air. But they went so far up into the clouds that the Medicine Men could not see the end of them. At length they returned to the village, and everyone was very sad about the little girl. They believed that they would never see her again.

The hunter was a very hardworking man. He loved little Umuk dearly. He asked all the Medicine Men whether they knew how he might find his daughter. Although they sang songs and danced strange dances, they could find no answer for him. At last he thought of the old grandmother of Niyak. She was very wise and almost as great as a Medicine Man. He talked with her.

"Yes," she said, "I think I can help you. I do not know just where little Umuk is. I can see a faraway place; but there is fog there, and I cannot see beyond it. If you will do just as I tell you, we'll try to find your little girl."

Then the old woman directed the hunter to make a pair of snowshoes for Niyak and an Eskimo walking stick so that he might feel his way over the ice and snow. She told the hunter that his wife should make a rainproof parka of seal and some gloves of fishskin. Then the orphan boy would not get wet in the land of the fog. Most important of all, she said, was a knapsack for him. It should be made of the skin of a swan with all the feathers on it.

35

When all these things were made for Niyak, the hunter and his wife took them to the old grandmother. Together with all the people of the village, they went to the Kashim, where there were two big drums made of walrus gut. The Medicine Men beat them with all their might.

The old grandmother asked for two large clamshells filled with food to be brought in. These were placed in the swanskin knapsack. Then Niyak was told to put on his new things, even the snowshoes, and to get ready to go in search of little Umuk. When he was fully dressed in the new rain parka and the fishskin gloves, he placed the knapsack on his back and stepped toward the porch of the Kashim. His feet did not even touch the floor. He walked out on the air while the drums played furiously.

Outside, Niyak, walking on air, came up to the window in the top of the Kashim. He stood upon the thin membrane of walrus skin that made the window. The people inside looked up at him. Suddenly he bounded upward into the sky and disappeared.

Going to the hill where Umuk had been lost, Niyak saw her tracks leading to the sky. He followed them easily until he came to the clouds. Then he went beyond the clouds. Soon he saw a door in the sky. It was like a door in an igloo. He opened it and looked inside. There he saw a very beautiful land with many pretty lakes, which had salmonberries growing all around the edges of them. He did not see any people. When he looked for the tracks of little Umuk, he saw them going on up into the sky.

Niyak followed the tracks of little Umuk. He could step right in them, for they were just the size for him. But as he looked closely, he saw that they were not the girl's tracks but larger ones. After following these larger tracks far up into the sky, he came to a door. He opened it and looked in.

Here he saw a land more beautiful than the last one. It was the most cheerful place Niyak had ever seen. There were lakes of blue water and salmonberries everywhere. A warm sun was shining and many birds were singing. He looked for the tracks he had been following. He found them going straight on up into the heavens. They were still the same tracks, so Niyak followed them.

Upward climbed the little orphan boy until, in the very top of the sky, he came to another door. It was closed. He opened it and looked in. There was nothing before his eyes but fog. He could not see two steps in front of him, and he could not see the tracks that he had followed so far.

37

"Here," he said to himself, "is as far as grandmother could see. She could not see beyond the fog. I wonder what I must do now."

Suddenly Niyak felt something move on his back. It was his swanskin knapsack.

"K-l-o-o-k, k-l-o-o-k," it said. "I will help you, little Niyak." The swan came down from Niyak's back and looked at the ground in the land of fog.

"Here are the tracks," the swan said. "You must follow them, and I will stay here and direct you. When you hear me call, you will know that you have lost the tracks and are not following them any more."

So Niyak started through the wet fog. He felt his way with the stick Umuk's father had made for him. He was very glad to have the fishskin gloves and the rain parka. It was very cold and wet. He could not see a thing. Suddenly he heard the swan say, "K-l-o-o-k." He knew he was not following the tracks, so he turned to the right and heard the swan no more. He went on for some distance and then heard the swan again. It was far away, but Niyak turned to the left this time. He listened for the swan but could not hear him. He went on. All at once he almost ran into a door just ahead of him. He opened it and looked in.

Here he beheld a land even more beautiful than any

he had ever seen. There were blue lakes with thousands of salmonberries growing on their shores. The sun shone warmly in the sky, and there were many trees with fruits of all colors on them. He looked for the tracks but could see none. So he walked along and looked at the beautiful trees and fruits. After walking for a long time, he saw in the distance a funny-looking tree. It was short and flat-looking on top. He went closer to see it. When he got very near, Niyak saw that the flat top was a giant bird's nest, and he climbed up to look at it.

Much to little Niyak's surprise, he found himself peering into a nest with five eagles in it. One of them was very tiny, and growing on his wings were feathers of all the colors in the world. The orphan boy thought it was the most beautiful little bird he had ever seen. The other eagles were larger, and all were of different sizes. The largest had all his feathers and looked big enough to fly. Only the smallest one had the beautiful colored feathers.

The eagles' nest was not very clean. Niyak decided that he would clean their house for them. He moved them to one side and took out all the old eggshells and bits of food they had not eaten. In the bottom of the nest, he felt a lot of old wet leaves. He threw them out, too. As he picked up the last of the leaves, he felt something round beneath his hand. It felt like someone's head. Lifting it up, he found it was little Umuk buried in the eagles' nest. She was alive but very weak and hungry.

Niyak was amazed. Quickly he climbed down from the nest with the little girl and placed her on the soft grass beneath a tree. He took out his two clamshells filled with food and fed her. Soon she felt better. As they talked they heard a queer loud noise like the tearing of heavy cloth. A giant eagle whizzed down from the sky, alighting on the edge of his nest. He looked around in the nest. Then he lifted up the front of his great hooked beak and took the skin from his face like a mask.

The eagle was a man. He spoke. "I want to thank whoever came here and cleaned up my nest," he said. "Please come out where I can see you. I will not harm you."

Niyak and Umuk stepped out from under the tree, and the eagle spoke to them. "You may take the little girl with you. Because you have cleaned my nest so nicely, I will give you one of my eagle children. Every time one of my children is born, I always get the baby a person for a pillow. That is why I took the little girl. You may have her back now and one of my little eagles besides."

Little Niyak was very glad to get a little eagle, for he

had always wanted one. "I would like to have the baby eagle," he told the father, "the little one with all the pretty feathers on him just like yours."

The father looked sad. "I would rather not let you have this little eagle," he said. "I am very fond of him. But as I have made you a promise, you shall have him. However, you must not take him with you now. He is so small that I must first raise him and teach him to fly. You go back to the earth. Five years from today I will bring this baby eagle to you. I must warn you never to let any person on earth see him, or he will come back to me and you will not have him any more. I want to keep this eagle and would much rather you took one of the others. This one is going to be just like me. The rest are like their mother."

So little Niyak took the girl, put her inside his parka, and set off for the earth world again. Soon they came to the door in the most beautiful land. They opened it. It was so foggy that little Niyak could not see a thing. He closed the door behind him, wondering how he would ever find his way. Suddenly he heard something very far away. He listened and heard it again.

"K-l-o-o-k, k-l-o-o-k." It was the swan calling him, showing him the way to go. Hastily the orphan boy set off in the direction of the voice. Soon it became louder.

At last Niyak came to the big white swan perched on a hummock of grass right by the door that led into the next beautiful land.

"Thank you so much," Niyak told the swan. "I have little Umuk here in my parka. We are going back to the world below. Do you want to go with us?"

"No," replied the swan. "I shall stay here. If any other people come this way, I will direct them through the land of the fog as I directed you. I will always give them good weather."

Niyak bade the bird good-bye and opened the door into the beautiful land. He could plainly see the tracks in the sky where he had been before. On he went, down through the last door, and at last saw the little hill where he and Umuk had picked the grass. He hurried on to the village. He could hear the drums in the Kashim. He opened the door and walked in. His snowshoes did not touch the floor, for he walked on the air.

The drums stopped beating and the people looked at the orphan boy. Beneath his parka they could see two little boots sticking out. He walked around the Kashim, circling in the air until he came to the hunter and his wife. Reaching beneath his parka, he took out little Umuk and handed her to her mother. She was very thin but well and happy.

All the people rejoiced at the return of Niyak and

Umuk. Great feasts were held in the Kashim for the two children. Games were played. The Medicine Men sang their best songs and did their best tricks. Everyone was very happy. After a while the people went about their regular duties again and everything was as it had been before.

Little Niyak did not forget the promise the eagle had made him. He kept track of the time very carefully. At the end of five years he went away from the village where no one could see him and watched for two days. He saw nothing and returned to his home again. The next day he went out, and the next. The eagle did not appear. Niyak wondered whether he had forgotten his promise.

The next day was bright and fine. Niyak walked far from the village and sat down on the tundra. He had not been there long when he saw two large clouds in the sky. They seemed to be moving closer to him. As the clouds drew nearer, he saw they were not clouds at all but two great eagles. They were the same size, and on their wings were the beautiful feathers.

One of the eagles carried a giant mukluk in one of his talons. In the other he held a deer. Both of these he dropped just in front of Niyak, and then both eagles alighted on the ground beside him.

Lifting back his face like a mask, the same man Niyak

had seen five years before spoke to him: "I am bringing you my son as I promised. He is just like me. Every day he will hunt for you. He will bring you more game than you can eat. You must remember always to come far out from the village to meet him. If anyone sees him, you will never see him again." Then both the eagles flew away, and Niyak took the fine deer and the mukluk, or seal, home.

The following day Niyak walked far out from the village and sat down. Soon the eagle appeared, carrying a spotted seal for him. He dropped it at Niyak's feet without a word and flew away. The orphan boy took the seal home. After that, anytime he wanted meat he walked far out from the village and the eagle brought it to him. Sometimes it would be a deer or a seal. The eagle was so big and powerful that he even brought Niyak a walrus or a whale once in a while.

Everyone in the village said that Niyak must be a great hunter. He married the girl he had rescued five years before, and they were very happy. The orphan was also a Medicine Man, and Umuk was a Medicine Woman. Her medicine was not quite as strong as that of Niyak because he had carried her beneath his parka. That made her weaker than he was.

One day as Niyak walked out to meet the eagle, he said to himself, "Why should I walk so far? I have to carry the animals which my eagle catches for me that much farther, and they are very heavy." So he sat down on the ground much closer to the village than ever before. Soon he saw the eagle coming.

It swooped down low and dropped a fat caribou at Niyak's feet, but the bird did not touch the ground. As he flew away, a man in the village looked up and saw the eagle. He called out to all the people. They ran out of their igloos and looked as the giant bird flew away.

Niyak picked up his meat and carried it home. It was not nearly so far as he usually had to walk. "This is much better," he said to himself, "than walking so far and carrying the heavy meat."

The next time Niyak needed meat, he walked out from the village and sat down. Soon he saw not only his eagle approaching but another who looked just like him. They alighted near him on the ground.

One of them lifted up his face like a mask. It was the man. He spoke. "You broke your promise to me and did not go far from the village. The people there saw my son, so he will never come back to you again."

Together the two eagles flew away.

Niyak went away from the village several times when he was hungry. He sat down and waited, but the eagle did not return. After that he had to hunt on foot as did the other Eskimos. He worked much harder than he had ever worked before. He and Umuk had five strong children, and they needed a great deal to eat.

Although this happened many, many years ago, before the white men ever came to Alaska, even today when an Eskimo breaks his promise the others will often say to him, "Remember how Niyak broke his promise because he was too lazy to walk far? He had to work hard all the rest of his life!"

Even in Eskimo land it is very bad to break a promise.

Chanimun

Why the Wolves Eat
As They Do

ONCE upon a time, a very long while before the white men came to Alaska, there lived five brothers and a sister. They had no mother or father and could not remember seeing them. The brothers were great hunters, but the sister was a naughty girl. In those days there were Indians who fought the Eskimo people, and there were fierce animals that would harm anyone they could catch. So the five brothers instructed their sister never to leave the igloo. She must stay close to their home, they told her, or she would be in danger.

The sister's name was Tuchung. She disobeyed her

47

brothers. Instead of staying near her igloo, as all Eskimo girls are supposed to do, she often wandered quite far from home. Sometimes she did not get supper for her brothers when they came home tired and hungry. She had a little dog called Gazok, and he went everywhere with her. He was just a puppy, born the autumn before, and this spring he was only about half-grown.

One day the five brothers told their sister that they were going to the ocean to hunt seals and that she should be sure to stay close to home. They told her that it would be most dangerous for her to go far from her igloo that day. As soon as her brothers had left, naughty Tuchung went out on the hill behind the igloo. The puppy went with her, for he was lonely when he stayed in the igloo by himself.

"Come, Gazok," cried Tuchung, "let us go on over to that other hill." And away she went, farther than ever. The puppy looked after her and whined. He knew that it was wrong for them to leave their home. But at last he followed.

Tuchung did not stop when she got to the hill but walked on and on. The puppy was frightened because she was disobeying, and he would not follow. Suddenly, as the girl went on, she heard the sound of singing coming from the direction of the ocean. She listened and was surprised to hear that it was addressed to her:

48

Tuchung, you should be at home.
Go back fast as you can,
Or something's going to catch you,
A wolf, or bear, or a man.
Aw-oo-oo-oo, aw-oo-oo-oo, aw-oo-oo-oo.

But the girl did not take warning and return at once to her igloo. "I do not see anything to bother me," she told herself. "But I wonder who it was singing. The last verse sounded like dogs howling."

Then as she wandered on, looking for blackberries, she heard the song again. It was closer this time and again came from the direction of the ocean:

We left today your brothers,
But now we're wolves so wild
That we will try to eat you
Or any other child.
Aw-oo-oo-oo, aw-oo-oo-oo, aw-oo-oo-oo.

Tuchung was a little disturbed by this and thought she had better start for home. Her brothers might return, and they would be angry to find her gone. But she did not hurry; she walked back slowly, stopping to pick a blackberry now and then. All of a sudden she heard the sound of running feet. Looking up, she saw five wolves coming toward her. Now she was badly fright-

49

ened and began to run, but she was far from home. Little Gazok, watching from the distant hill, howled dismally. There was nothing he could do, but he started toward Tuchung to help her.

The wolves rushed up to her, and the leader spoke. "Why did you not do as you were told and stay at home?" he demanded. "Now we must eat you, for we are wolves." With that he lifted his hood and Tuchung saw that it was her eldest brother. Quickly he pulled the terrible wolfskin back over his face. Then the five beasts sprang upon the poor girl and devoured her.

Little Gazok was still running toward the wolves when they went off toward the mountains in the east. He hurried to the spot where Tuchung had been and saw what had happened.

"Now my mistress is gone," the puppy whined. "There will be no one to feed me, and I shall have to stay in the igloo all by myself. I must follow the wolves if I am to have anything to eat. Maybe if I sing to them they will leave me something when they kill." Hurrying after them as fast as his short legs would take him, Gazok began to sing:

> Oh save some scraps for me, big wolves.
> I'm such a tiny mite,
> I'll starve if I do not get food.
> Please save me just a bite.

On ran the puppy after the five wolves. He saw them far ahead going over a distant hill. When he got to the top of that hill, he saw them still farther ahead just going over another one. On he ran to the top of that hill. When he got there he could not see them. So he put his puppy nose to the ground and followed the scent of their tracks. He followed for a long time, and just as he was about to give up he came to the top of a little mound. There, just ahead, he saw the five wolves with a caribou they had killed. Beyond them he could see a village.

As little Gazok drew closer, he saw something that greatly surprised him. The wolves took off their skins and were the five brothers of Tuchung. He went up to them wagging his tail.

"We heard you singing, little dog," the oldest brother said. "If you want meat you must go to yonder village and borrow a knife and a stone to sharpen it. Then we will cut up the caribou and give you some."

Little Gazok hurried as fast as he could to the village and went into the first house. There were several men there. He asked as politely as he could whether he might borrow a knife and a whetstone. They looked at him coldly and said, "You killed the caribou; use your own tools. We have none to lend to strangers." And all over the village the little dog asked for a knife and a sharpening stone. But no one would lend him one. At length he went back to the hill where the five brothers were waiting.

"I could not get the knife and the whetstone at the village," he told them. "They would not let me have their tools."

"Then the people will be sorry they were so selfish. If we have no knife to cut up the caribou, then we must eat it like wolves."

So the leader and his brothers put on their wolfskins again and fell to devouring the caribou like wolves. When they had finished they left some for little Gazok. He ate heartily as the five wolves loped away.

After the puppy had eaten, he went to the village, for he had no other home. A nice little girl let him live with her and her parents. He told the people what the leader of the wolves had said. They were ashamed that they had been so selfish. To this day the Eskimo people believe that there are still wolves in the world because long ago the selfish village people would not lend the five brothers a knife and a whetstone to cut up their caribou.

Chanimun

Agayk and the Dwarf

A YOUNG man named Agayk once lived with his wife by a little river near the Kashunuk village. This was ages ago, long before the white men came to Alaska. Agayk was an orphan, and in those days children raised without their parents often saw elves, dwarfs, and fairies that other people and children couldn't see. Elves were always nice. Dwarfs were ugly and bad and always up to some mischief.

Agayk was strong and a good hunter. He had two igloos—one for winter, when he hunted caribou, and one for the summer months, when he fished for salmon and other fish. His good wife gathered salmonberries in the warm weather and mixed them with seal oil and put them into a sealskin poke for their winter food. A sealskin poke is just like a big bag made of leather, and Eskimo people use them for the storing of their food and even their personal belongings.

One spring, just before Agayk and his wife moved from their winter igloo to their summer place, a strange thing happened. The young man had some basket traps set in a little creek to catch blackfish and needlefish. One morning, as he went to them, he saw someone taking the fish out of the trap.

"Stop!" he called to the person. "You must not take my fish. If you do, my wife and I will have nothing to eat." With that, he ran very fast toward the fish thief. As he ran he saw that it was a dwarf. The dwarf began to run away.

Agayk was young and strong and afraid of nothing. He chased the dwarf as hard as he could.

The dwarf's arms were so long that the sleeves of his kuspuk dragged on the ground. But those sleeves were so full of needlefish and blackfish that they were heavy and dragged far behind him.

Agayk was sure he could catch the dwarf because of all the fish in his sleeves. The little man ran straight toward a hill. Agayk gained on him. Just as they got to the side of the hill, the young man reached out to catch the dwarf, but the queer little fellow ran right into the side of the hill and disappeared into the earth. There was no hole there or any place that Agayk could get into to fetch him out.

The young man went back to his winter igloo and then, with his wife, moved to their summer fishing place. They stayed there several days.

Then Agayk's wife said, "I wish you would go back to our winter igloo and bring me my sealskin poke. There are a lot of sinews and needles in it that I need badly."

So the next day the young man set out for his winter igloo. It was quite a long journey, and when he got there it was night and very dark.

He lit his seal-oil lamp and cooked his supper. Then he went to bed. He wanted a good sleep before returning to the summer fishing place with his wife's sealskin poke. He had no more than fallen asleep when he was awakened by someone shaking him.

Drowsily he rolled over, but he could see nothing. The inside of the igloo was as black as could be.

"Wake up," a rough voice was saying. "I am the dwarf you tried to catch. I have come back to fight you."

With that, the cruel dwarf caught Agayk by his long black hair and dragged him onto the floor. Then he started pounding the young man with some kind of club.

Agayk was very brave. He was strong, too. In the

dark he struck back at the terrible dwarf with his fists. But the dwarf, with his club, was on top of Agayk, so he could do little. Groping on the floor in the dark for something to fight with, Agayk felt the lid of a heavy earthenware cooking pot. He grasped that and brought it down as hard as he could right on the peaked head of the dwarf.

The nasty dwarf grunted, and Agayk felt him shudder. Then the young man rolled over on top of him just like little boys do when they are wrestling. Pushing with all his might, Agayk shoved the dwarf right down into the floor of the igloo. He pushed so hard that the dwarf went clear out of sight into the earth and was never seen again.

That was the last dwarf ever seen in Alaska. Even the orphan children never saw another, and they see many things that other people do not.

The Wicked Old Man
of the Sea

Many years ago the Eskimos at Hooper Bay were plagued by a wicked Old Man of the Sea. Often at night, as the people looked out from their igloos toward the ocean, they would see a round ball of fire. It would come up out of the waves, remain there for several minutes, and then disappear. This was the Old Man of the Sea, and the people would be afraid. When he appeared it was a sign that someone would drown.

Usually the seal hunters in their tiny kayaks would

be the ones who were taken. A man would fail to return after the ball of fire had been seen upon the ocean.

Not all the Eskimo people would see the ball of fire. Many of them did, but those who saw it most often were the little orphan children. They seemed to have a gift for seeing such things. People always said the orphan children were much cleverer than other children. Sometimes they were even wiser than the old people. In ancient times, these orphans often lived alone, apart from the rest of the village. Probably they had more time to think and to see things that the other children, who played all the time, were too busy to see.

Near the Hooper Bay village lived two little orphan brothers. One was eleven years old. His name was John. His little brother was nine, and his name was Joe. They were good children and spent most of their time looking out toward the sea while the other children were playing. Several times they saw the round ball of fire come up out of the waves and warned the people to be careful. Nevertheless, someone was always drowned.

Quite late one night, several of the Eskimo children in the village were playing in an igloo. They were very noisy and would not go to bed. It was long past the time when good little Eskimos were supposed to be asleep, too. Several of the parents had told them to stop playing, but they paid no attention at all.

The little orphan brothers, John and Joe, were looking out to sea. They were not playing with the other children. Suddenly they saw the big ball of fire come up on top of the waves. It was very bright and angry. It seemed to be coming toward the village. Swiftly they ran to warn the people and to tell them what they saw. They stopped at the igloo where the noisy children were playing and told them to be careful because the Old Man of the Sea was coming.

The noisy children did not listen to what John and Joe told them. They went right on playing, making more noise than ever. The orphan boys went up on the hill to look again. Sure enough, the ball of fire was getting closer. They ran into the igloo where the children were playing and told them to rush home. The Old Man of the Sea was really coming to the village.

This time the bad children laughed at the orphan boys and told them the Old Man never came into the village. They said John and Joe were "fraidy-cats." They went right on playing their noisy games. Joe tried to push some of the little boys out of doors to see for themselves, but they refused to be alarmed.

Suddenly there was a roar like a great gust of wind and the igloo lit up as bright as day. Then the bad children were frightened. They knew the Old Man was just outside. He came onto the porch of the igloo but was so big he could not get in. Everyone felt a little better. The boys and girls crouched in the corners, hoping he could not reach them.

Then the door was pushed open and the Old Man reached in with his big hand. It was a most terrible hand. Each finger had a mouth with sharp teeth in it. And in the palm of the hand was the largest mouth of all, with the longest, sharpest teeth. The children stared at it in terror.

The hand groped around all over the igloo and the fingers with mouths on them caught the bad little children and devoured them. The poor orphans were terribly frightened, but they were cleverer than the other children. Little Joe found a big sealskin on the floor and rolled up in it. Whenever the awful hand reached out to catch him, he would go rolling across the floor out of the way.

John found a large wooden dish that the Eskimos used for eating berries. It is called a kantak. He pulled the large dish over himself and it covered him up just like a turtle shell. Whenever the Old Man's hand would feel the wooden dish, it would turn away, for it did not know there was a little Eskimo boy beneath it.

After all the children except John and Joe had been eaten by the hand, the Old Man went away. The orphans ran to the door of the igloo and watched the big ball of fire as it rolled back to the sea and then went beneath the waves.

All the people of the village grieved for the poor children who had been eaten by the Old Man of the Sea, even though they had been naughty and had not gone to bed when they should. The orphans said they thought they could make a trap to catch the Old Man of the Sea. All the men of the village said they would help if the boys would only tell them what to do.

The orphans told the men to hang in the porch of the igloo a great big heavy iron knife that had been made from the rudder of a ship. This weighed almost a hundred pounds. They sharpened the edge of this knife with their files until it was as keen as a razor. Then they hung the knife right over the door and tied great heavy rocks to the top of it so that when they cut the rope that held it, the knife would fall across the doorsill and the heavy rocks would drive it deep into the monster hand.

John tried the knife on a heavy stick almost as thick as a man's arm and it cut clean through. They were sure that if the Old Man came again, they would surprise him and perhaps kill him, so that no one would ever be eaten again.

The first night after the trap had been fixed, more children came to play in the igloo. They shouted and played until late at night, hoping to attract the Old Man of the Sea. But he did not appear. The next night, too, the children played and the orphan boys kept watch.

The Old Man of the Sea did not come that night, either.

On the third night, the children played more noisily than ever. Joe and John kept watch from the hill. The children played on far into the night, and several men who were in the igloo with them to help fight the Old Man of the Sea became drowsy and wanted to go home. Just as they were about to give up and go to bed, one of the orphan boys looked out to sea and there on the waves was the round ball of fire. It was heading straight toward the village.

They ran to the igloo and told the men to get ready. The Old Man was coming again. The people were afraid, but they waited; and the children went on shouting and playing as if they did not know that the horrible Old Man was about to arrive. Little Joe stood by the doorway with his hunting knife ready to cut the rope if the Old Man put his hand through the door again. Then came the roar of the wind and the igloo lit up again. The Old Man of the Sea had arrived.

This time, instead of coming to the doorway, he went to the window in the top of the igloo and started to reach in through it. The people were afraid that he had found out about the trap, but John called out to him, "Old Man of the Sea, you cannot come in through the window. Come in through the door as you did before."

The terrible huge hand left the window. In a moment

the door was pushed open and in came the groping hand with the wicked mouths on each finger and the big mouth and the long sharp teeth in the palm. All the men grasped their hunting knives, and all the little children backed away into the far corners of the igloo. Then the fingers began to grope about, trying to catch a child. When all the hand was through the doorway, Joe cut the rope with his knife.

Down fell the heavy knife with the rocks on top of it. The terrible hand, cut free, came wriggling into the room with the horrible mouths snapping at everything. At once the men sprang forward and cut it into tiny pieces. Then they tried to open the door, but they could not get out. They did not see the light again, nor did they hear the roar of the wind. All was quiet outside.

When daylight came, some of the men boosted little Joe up through the window in the top of the igloo. He went around to the porch to see why they could not get out. Blocking the doorway was a big iceberg, filling up the whole entrance to the igloo. The Old Man of the Sea had turned to solid ice.

Since that day a long, long time ago, the Eskimo people of Hooper Bay have never been bothered by the Old Man of the Sea. They say he had a wife, and some-times, maybe once a year, they can see her come up on top of the waves in a round ball of fire, as did her husband. The ball of fire is not as large as it was when her husband was alive because she is smaller and not quite so wicked. Often after the Old Woman of the Sea is seen, a hunter may drown in his kayak, but little children are no longer noisy in the igloos at night.

Occasionally, when it is getting late at Hooper Bay and children are playing in the igloo, their parents will say, "Run along to bed now, children. Remember how the Old Man of the Sea came a long time ago when the little boys and girls did not obey? Maybe his wife will not like it if you stay up too late."

Then the little children will scamper off as fast as they can. They will look out toward the Bering Sea to see whether the ball of fire is by any chance floating on the waves. They seldom see it, and then only if they have been very, very bad.

The Orphan Boys
and the Clapping Mountains

At Hooper Bay lived two orphans, John and Joe. It was they who saw the great ball of fire when the wicked Old Man of the Sea came to their village. As the orphan boys grew older, everyone said that they would be great Medicine Men because they were so clever. They could see many things that other people could not see. So they made long journeys to gain more knowledge of the world, which would make them great Medicine Men, able to help the people at Hooper Bay.

They met an old Eskimo man and an old Eskimo woman when they were traveling on the Kashunuk River. They told the orphans how they had once raised a pair of Canada geese named Twaddles and Waddles and how they learned to speak their language. These geese migrated south one winter and returned in the spring with a strange tale of mountains that clapped together. It seemed that somewhere downstream were mountains that came slap together whenever a bird attempted to fly between them.

The orphans were very interested and decided that they must see for themselves whether such a thing was true. They knew that often the ducks and geese became quite scarce at Hooper Bay and always used to wonder why this was. Taking two kayaks, they set out one bright summer day to find the mountains that clapped together.

For days the orphan boys paddled. They went past Nunivak Island, where the wicked Medicine Men lived who had killed the "Never Sleepy Man." They passed it far out to sea and watched the channel beyond the beautiful harbor to be sure some witchcraft was not played on them. Then they went on beyond the mouth of the Kuskokwim. One evening they saw two mountains close together. Suddenly these crashed against each other with a terrific force. The boys knew that at last they were in the land of the Clapping Mountains. However, they were not afraid.

When morning came, they paddled in their kayaks very close to the mountains so that they could get a good look at these treacherous things that closed on every bird or man who tried to pass between them. They did not at once try to go between them, but very carefully stopped just outside to look and learn more about them. Instead of flying through as fast as they could without looking, as the birds had done, they first gazed up at the sides of the mountains. What they saw there greatly astonished John and Joe.

On each side of the terrible mountains there were faces in the rock, and the boys could see that the faces were watching them. All of them were scowling and were very ugly. They seemed to be very curious about the orphan boys. They had clearly never seen people before.

"Let us go through the Clapping Mountains," said John, the older boy. "I think we can paddle our kayaks right through without getting caught."

"How can we do that?" Joe asked his brother. "The faces are watching. As soon as we get into the stream between the mountains, they will clap together and catch us."

"We will put up our little tent," said John. "Then

we will dress up as comically as we can. We'll jump into our kayaks and paddle straight between the mountains. They will be so surprised to see us in our funny costumes, they will forget to clap together."

The orphan boys put up their little tent on a sandbar in the river that flowed between the Clapping Mountains. They took off their beautiful parkas and turned them inside out. John tied a bunch of eagle feathers over his face so that the faces on the mountains could not see him. Joe hung tails of the red fox from his cap. Really, they looked very strange and not at all like two boys. When they were all ready they ran out of their tent, jumped into their kayaks, and paddled straight through the Clapping Mountains.

John peered out through his eagle feathers. He saw the faces watching them. They looked very surprised. As they went on through the mountains, the boys could see the faces, screwed up in the most perplexed manner, all along the way. They could not recognize the two strange things paddling between them. All of a sudden the orphan boys saw there were no more mountains. They had gone between them. Then they laughed to think how they had fooled the faces into watching them so intently that they forgot to clap together.

The two orphan boys traveled on, visiting the beautiful land beyond the Clapping Mountains. Everywhere there were big salmonberries, the biggest John and Joe had ever seen. They caught great fish, much bigger than the salmon, and roasted them over the fire at night. It was a very pleasant land, and it did not rain every day as it did at Hooper Bay.

One night, as they were finishing their supper of salmonberries and fish, John said, "We had better be starting back on our journey, for it is a long one. We have already been away from Hooper Bay for a month. Our people will become worried about us."

"I know we should," said little Joe, "but we must go back between the Clapping Mountains again. I'm afraid we cannot fool them so easily this time."

"We will go to the mountains in the night," John told his brother. "We'll hide behind the big rocks there and dress up differently than we did before. Maybe we can fool the faces again. While they are looking at us, we can pass between them."

After dark the next evening, the orphan boys paddled up behind the big rocks. They were sure the faces had not seen them. Quickly they disguised themselves in every way that they could think of. Over their kayaks they tied green willow branches so that when the faces looked down they would see no kayak at all, just the green branches being paddled along. Then the boys took red clay and painted their faces. They tied bundles of grass to their kayak paddles so that the faces on the cliffs would not see the paddles at all.

Little Joe took his tea pail and made a funny hat of it. On it he tied a wolf tail. It fluttered in the breeze and looked for all the world as if a wolf had crawled into the tea pail with just his tail sticking out. John took the skin of a loon and tied it on his head like a cap with a big red handkerchief. It looked just as if a loon had been tied fast to the green willows that covered John's kayak. He knew the faces would not be able to understand such a queer-looking thing.

When day broke, John spoke to little Joe: "Now, let us go. Do not be afraid. Follow close behind me with your kayak. While the faces are busy looking at us, we will go safely between them." Off they paddled. John could see the faces staring down at them in astonishment.

On they went. Just as they were about to come out from between the Clapping Mountains, little Joe looked up at the faces. At the same moment there was a great gust of wind between the rocky walls. Off sailed the tea pail from Joe's head. He was very frightened. Looking up, he saw the faces nod to one another. The mountains started to tremble. He paddled as hard as he could. Then, with a deafening noise, the mountains clapped together.

John had already got through, and all of little Joe's kayak except the stern was through. When the mountains came together, they caught the stern of his kayak and held it fast. But little Joe was safe.

Swiftly the orphan boy reached for his hunting knife. Quickly he cut off the tail of the little boat right up against the rocks that held it so tight. John paddled up beside him in his kayak, and Joe got in with his brother. He held on to the little kayak without the tail even though it filled with water and almost sank. Rapidly, John paddled away and stopped over at the sandbar. Their tent still stood where they had left it many days ago.

John looked back at the faces and laughed. They were all scowling fiercely. It was easy to see they were very angry because the boys had escaped from them a second time.

"Now," said John, "we must fix your kayak again and start back for our home at Hooper Bay." The boys took bone needles and stout string made of whale sinew and sewed a new stern on little Joe's kayak. When they had finished, they greased the new seams with seal oil. The little kayak did not leak a drop.

Together the orphan boys paddled back past the Kuskokwim River. Very cautiously they went around Nunivak Island, where the bad Medicine Men lived.

When they came to the Kashunuk River, they stopped and stayed all night with the old Eskimo man and the old Eskimo woman and told them of their adventures. These two were greatly excited by the story and were pleased that the orphan boys had gone to look at the Clapping Mountains. Now they knew that Twaddles and Waddles had told the truth.

Then John and Joe returned to Hooper Bay. They told the people that they had been through the Clapping Mountains. Everyone was more certain than ever that the orphans would grow up to be great Medicine Men. When John and Joe told the people how they had fooled the faces by making them so curious that they forgot to clap together, the Eskimos all laughed. They asked Joe and John to dress up for them just as they had for the faces so that they could see how funny they looked.

But the Eskimo people never go too far from Hooper Bay in their kayaks because they do not wish to go between the Clapping Mountains. It is a good thing the orphan boys found out about them. If the faces had not been so curious, the orphan boys might not have returned home again.

"It is not good to be too curious, like the faces, and stare too long at anything when you wish to catch it," the Eskimos say. "And besides it is not very polite."

The Wolves
and the Caribou Woman

ONCE upon a time, before the white men came to Alaska, there was a woman who lived all alone at Hooper Bay. She had no parents, nor had she a husband or children. She was very poor. There was no way for her to earn money. Even today the Eskimo people have hardly any money to buy groceries. Instead they must hunt seals, catch fish, and scour the tundra to find greens in the lakes. Sometimes they find mouse food. It is really difficult for the people at Hooper Bay to get enough to eat.

The poor woman had a difficult time finding food. All during the summer months she had barely enough to keep her alive. When winter came she had nothing at all to eat in her igloo. One cold winter day she went out to a little stream near Hooper Bay. With a bone ice chisel she cut a hole in the ice and piled the cakes of ice beside her. She had a small sled on which she hauled her fishing gear. She propped the sled up beside her and spread an old grass mat over all of it to make a windbreak. Eskimo people always do this when they are fishing or sitting in their kayaks on the edge of the ice watching for seals. They put up a grass mat or a piece of canvas to keep off the wind. Even then it is very cold.

For her fishing, the woman used an Eskimo tomcod net. This was a triangle made of three sticks tied together, with a netting made of white whale sinews fastened to them. It looked like a three-cornered bag. One of the sticks was longer than the others and was the handle of the net. The poor woman sat by the ice and kept dipping her net down into the water. Occasionally she would catch a tomcod.

While she was fishing, she looked across the tundra and saw a caribou. The animal was running hard and seemed very frightened. It came right up to the woman and stopped close beside her. The woman was astonished that a wild animal should come so close to her. She was even more astonished when the caribou reached up with a forefoot and pulled back the skin of its face. Inside there was a woman.

"Oh, please help me," she cried. "There are wolves after me, and I can run no farther. Please tell me what I can do to escape them."

"I will hide you, you poor thing," the Eskimo woman said. With her wooden shovel she made a hole among the cakes of ice. "Jump in here," she told the caribou.

The caribou got into the hole in the middle of the ice cakes as quickly as she could. The poor woman covered her with the mat. No sooner was the caribou hidden than the Eskimo woman heard wolves howling. Looking across the tundra, she saw five of them swiftly following the tracks of the caribou. They came right up to the poor woman and stopped.

The leader of the wolves then did a very astonishing thing. He reached up with his front foot and pulled back the skin from his face. He was a man. "Tell me," he said, "if you have seen a caribou come this way. My four brothers and I have followed her for miles."

"Yes," replied the poor woman. "I saw a caribou running like the wind. She came right past here and went toward the mountains yonder. She must be very far away by now."

The leader of the wolves quickly pulled his wolf face into place again. He walked right by the blocks of ice where the caribou woman was hiding. The poor woman shook with fright because she feared that the wolf might scent the animal covered with the grass mat. But he did not. Away the wolves went, in full cry, as fast as they could.

The poor old woman went on with her fishing, and the caribou woman remained hidden. Before long, from far across the tundra, the woman heard singing. There, running less swiftly than the five wolf brothers, came an old wolf. As he ran he kept time to the sound of his galloping feet on the frozen snow by singing this song:

> *I am old and can run no more;*
> *My teeth are worn, and my paws are sore.*
> *I'll follow my five sons over the hill*
> *And eat the caribou that they kill.*
> *Aw-oo-oo-oo, aw-oo-oo-oo.*

The poor old woman trembled with fear when she heard this old wolf singing. The caribou woman hiding in the ice cakes under the grass mat shook, too. But the wolf ran on, following the tracks of his five sons toward the hills. As he ran, he sang another verse:

> *The caribou's heart is very sweet;*
> *That is the first thing that I'll eat.*
> *I'll have steaks and ribs and eat my fill*
> *With my five sons far over the hill.*
> *Aw-oo-oo-oo, aw-oo-oo-oo.*

"Mercy," the poor woman said to the caribou woman, "how those bloodthirsty wolves make me shiver! And now, my dear," she said, uncovering the caribou woman, "you had better run back the way you came and you will be safe. The wolf brothers will never know you went in that direction."

"I do not know how to thank you for saving my life," the caribou woman said. Then she put her skin over her face again and was not a woman any more. As the poor woman looked, the caribou woman knelt down on the ice and seemed to pull her shiny hooves right inside of her legs, just like a little boy can pull his hands up into his sleeves. Reaching inside her skin, the queer animal pulled out a great pile of sweet caribou fat and gave it all to the poor old woman.

"Here is some delicious fat for you," she said, "and may you always have good luck with your fishing and always have plenty to eat." Then the caribou woman trotted away.

The poor woman was so glad to get the sweet caribou fat that she burst into tears. It was very cold, and Eskimo people need a great amount of fat in the wintertime to keep warm. She dipped her net again. It was so heavy she could hardly lift it. It was filled with tomcods! Soon she had all she could carry home on her little sled. It was enough to last her a long time.

Ever after, the poor woman caught all the fish she needed. In the summertime she always found lots of greens in the bottom of the lakes and large stores of mouse food and many berries. The Eskimo people say that she had such good luck because she had been kind to the caribou woman. That strange animal had made good medicine for the poor woman so that she would always have plenty of food.

It always pays to be kind, especially to animals.

Chaulimun

The Kashim of the Birds

A LONG time before the white men came to Alaska, a very poor man and his wife lived on the bank of the Kashunuk River. They were so poor that they lived on fish alone. The man had no spears or kayak or bow and arrows with which to hunt.

A tiny stream emptied into the Kashunuk where the man and his wife had their igloo. In this stream were many blackfish and needlefish. Both these fish are queer little things, hardly as large as the goldfish in your goldfish bowl. The blackfish were so small and thin that you could see the light right through them. The needlefish had tiny needles, or spines, on their backs and bellies and tail. The Eskimo people like to eat them, and many little boys and girls up near the Bering Sea would starve in the winter if it were not for these little fish.

The man caught the little fish in a basket trap. It was just a round basket made of thin willows, woven very tight. One end of the basket was closed like the bottom of an ordinary basket, and at the other end was a funnel made of willows with the big end outward. As the little fish swam up to the basket trap, they would be led into the open end of the funnel. Once they were in the basket they could not get out again. The inside end of the funnel was too small.

For many years the poor man and his wife lived by the little stream and caught blackfish and needlefish. Sometimes they would trade them to other Eskimos for seals and other animals that the hunters caught. Then one day in the spring the man went to his traps and there were hardly any fish in them at all. The next day he went again and found fewer fish than before.

"I cannot understand this," he told his wife. "I know there are lots of blackfish and needlefish in the little stream, but we do not catch them. I will watch my traps tomorrow and see what is the matter." So the man hid on a hill the next day and watched. At last he went to sleep.

How long he slept he did not know. Suddenly he

awoke and, looking toward his trap, saw someone taking the little fishes out of them. "I say," he called, "leave my traps alone! No wonder my wife and I have nothing to eat. You are robbing us."

He ran at top speed toward the traps. As he came closer, he saw that the robber was a crane. The crane had a walking stick, as all the Eskimos have, and he carried it with his wings. When he saw the man running toward him, he started to run and did not try to fly.

The man ran after the crane and soon was so close to him that he was just reaching out to catch him. But the crane said, "Kllurk, kllurk, kllurk," as all cranes do, and began to run faster. Again the man came up to the robber crane and was about to catch him by the tail. But again the crane cried, "Kllurk, kllurk, kllurk," and ran even faster than before. Every time the man would get close, the crane would sing his funny song and draw away from the man.

Cranes are funny birds and have a cry something like a swan's. They do it with two queer tubes in their breastbone that are like a trumpet. You can hear their clear, mellow notes for great distances.

This crane now began to seem tired, and the man felt sure that he would soon catch him. Suddenly he saw a village right ahead of him with a Kashim, or Man

House, very close by. The crane ran straight to the Man House, into the porch and out of sight.

"Now," said the man to himself, "I will catch that robber crane, for he went into the Kashim." But the man found the porch too narrow to get through.

Then the man climbed up on top of the Kashim where the window is. He peered through a crack into the Man House below. There he saw the robber crane lying on the floor. He appeared to be all out of breath. In fact, he seemed quite ill. The poor man looked further and gasped at what he saw. Inside the Kashim there were not people but birds. He saw emperor geese and king eider ducks and all the birds that live in Alaska sitting around in the Man House. They were all looking at the crane and talking very excitedly.

"I wonder what is the matter with our hunter?" he heard a big goose say. "He seems to be very ill. Hey, Crane, what is the matter with you?" But the crane could not answer, for he was out of breath from running.

"We should do something to make him well," said a big, dark cormorant. "We must have a Medicine Man sing over him. Whom shall we have for a Medicine Man?"

"Let's have the puffin for a Medicine Man," an eagle spoke up. "He can make very good medicine." So a puffin came from the north side of the Man House. He wore a feather on the very top of his head and seemed a very vain bird. A little duck took a drum from the wall and handed it to the puffin, who walked up to the side of the crane and began to sing:

> It is of the puffin people
> That you will hear me sing.
> They swim beneath the ocean
> And use both foot and wing.

The owl cleared his throat. He was very wise. "I don't think that is a good medicine song," he said. "The puffin is only bragging about himself."

Several other birds nodded their heads, for they thought the same thing. Then the puffin sang again as he played his drum:

> Upon the land they are quite smart;
> You'll find them very fleet,
> For when they run, they use their wings
> And also use their feet.

"That is very poor medicine," the old owl hooted quite angrily. "We do not want to hear how smart the puffins are. We want good medicine songs that will help the crane feel better. Let's have the white-fronted goose sing. He is very wise."

83

All the birds agreed with the old owl at the tops of their voices. So the puffin put the drum on the floor of the Man House, and the white-fronted goose came from the south side of the Kashim. He took the drum and, standing very straight, stretched his neck and looked right toward the window in the top of the Kashim.

He began to sing:

> *Oh, I see the eye of someone*
> *Looking at Mr. Crane.*
> *I'll poke him with my drumstick,*
> *And he'll not come again.*

With that, the white-fronted goose poked with his drumstick right up through the window in the top of the Kashim where the poor man was peering in. He poked him right in the eye. The shrewd goose had seen the man watching through the corner of the window.

The poor man on top of the Kashim saw a flash of fire. Something seemed to burn in his eyes. It hurt terribly when the white-fronted goose poked him with the drumstick. The man rolled off the Kashim and fainted.

How long the poor man was unconscious he did not know. At last he came to and sat up and looked around. He expected to see the village and Kashim where all the birds were, but he saw nothing. He rubbed his eyes. There were still tears in them because the drumstick had hurt very much. He looked north, south, east, and west, but he saw nothing of the village or the Kashim. All he saw was his basket traps and the little stream. He was back on top of the hill where he had been sitting as he watched the robber crane steal his fish.

The poor man looked back toward his igloo and saw his good wife waving to tell him that dinner was ready. He rubbed his sore eyes and wondered whether it had all been a dream. But he was sure it had not—he remembered so well chasing the robber crane.

To this day the Eskimo people around the Kashunuk River will tell you that there is a village and a great Kashim where the birds all live. If you do not believe them, they will tell you about the poor man who, many years before the white men came to Alaska, saw all the various birds in their Kashim. For the rest of his life the poor man always caught plenty of blackfish and needlefish. He believed that it was because the crane was afraid to ever come back and rob his traps again.

> *Sometimes you have dreams that are silly,*
> *And sometimes they seem to be true,*
> *But it's usually something you've eaten,*
> *When a dream ever comes to you.*

The Orphan Boy
and the Beavers

Many years ago an orphan boy named Niklik lived at Hooper Bay. His name was the same as that of the white-fronted goose. Everyone knows that this is one of the wisest birds. Like all orphans, this boy could see things and do things beyond the power of other children and even older people. One fine day, after the ice had thawed from the creeks and streams, Niklik set out on one of his greatest adventures.

He paddled his kayak up a winding creek that emptied into Hooper Bay. Soon he was in the hill country and far from any of his people. As the tiny kayak glided along, the boy suddenly saw a beautiful young woman by the bank of the stream. She was washing her hair and humming a little song. She had not seen the orphan boy.

"What a beautiful young woman," Niklik said to himself. "Maybe she would make me a good wife."

Quietly, as is the custom of the Eskimo people, he approached her and reached out to put his arms about her shoulders. For an instant the orphan boy closed his eyes, and when he opened them he was greatly surprised. Instead of a young woman, he held in his arms a tall, slender stalk of the wild celery plant that the Eskimos eat. It was an old, withered plant from the previous year.

"What can be the matter with me!" he exclaimed. "I must be imagining things."

He threw the old, dried plant into the water and paddled on. He had gone hardly a mile when he heard the beating of drums ahead of him. There on the bank of the river he saw a great many Eskimo women dancing while the men played the drums. Creeping closer to watch, Niklik listened to the music and admired the dancing. He closed his eyes for a second. When he opened them there were no people there. Instead there were a few slender willows nodding and swaying in the wind. The orphan boy rubbed his eyes. He could not believe that he had not seen people.

87

"What can be the matter with me?" he wondered, getting back into his kayak and paddling on. "I was sure I saw a dance and many people."

On he paddled for a long time. By now it was late in the night, but it was still light. In the Far North in the summertime it never really gets dark. Coming to a bend in the creek, the orphan boy saw a woman dancing. She was all alone and as she danced, she sang this song:

I'm all alone here by myself;
Someone should marry me.
I fish and sew and hunt and cook;
A fine wife I would be.

She was really lovely. As Niklik listened, he decided that she would make a fine wife. He got quietly out of his kayak, and the woman did not see him. Walking up behind her, the orphan boy put his arms about her. For a second he closed his eyes. When he opened them he was again surprised. In his arms was a wild celery plant. It was withered and dry from the year before. He pulled it up from the ground and threw it into the stream.

"I cannot understand all this," he told himself. "I was so sure I heard the young woman singing. I know that I saw her. There is some magic here."

He paddled on into the night. Just about the time the

sun peeked up, he looked ahead. In the distance he saw a
tree. He had come very far, for trees do not grow near
Hooper Bay. In the top of the tree sat an old gray-
haired man, and Niklik heard him singing:

> *Here come the Yukon warriors,*
> *In kayaks painted red.*
> *Run for your life, oh Niklik,*
> *Or soon now you'll be dead.*

"Gracious," gasped Niklik, "the Yukon warriors are
coming. I must run as fast as I can. How far are they?"
he called to the old man sitting in the tree. "Are they
very near?"

"Hoo—hoo—hoo," answered the old man in the
tree. Then out he flew, a big old owl.

Niklik gazed after him in astonishment. "There certainly is some magic here," he thought. "I was sure I
heard an old man singing about warriors."

He paddled on up the creek. As the sun came up, he
saw a beaver swimming. Paddling silently up toward
the animal, the orphan boy took his spear from his
kayak. Here was a fine fur he would have. Just as he
was going to throw his harpoon, the beaver turned and
saw him.

Holding up his paws in a friendly fashion, he spoke
to Niklik. "Do not throw that spear at me," he said. "I

am a little boy just like you." Then the beaver pulled back the hood of his fur parka and the face of a boy looked out.

How amazed Niklik was! "Are you the only person living here?" he asked. "Do you have your parents with you?"

"Oh, I am not alone," the little beaver answered in the Eskimo language. "I live with several people. I am the smallest," and he laughed, rather embarrassed. "They call me Tail Flapper."

How funnily the beaver talked. Niklik had never heard anyone with such a queer accent before. Then he spoke again to the beaver boy. "What do you mean by Tail Flapper? Why do they call you that?"

"We build dams in the streams," the little beaver said. "Everyone has some job. I am the Tail Flapper, and it is my job to flap my tail when I hear enemies coming. Sometimes I flap my tail and pat out the mud that the Mud Packer brings."

"Oh," said the orphan boy, "then there is a beaver called the Mud Packer, too, is there?"

"Yes," answered the little beaver, "and there is a Wood Cutter. He cuts the trees for the dam. Also there is the Wood Packer. He carries the wood to the dam when it is cut."

"Then there are four of you," said Niklik. "That is a fine way you people have—each one with his job."

"Oh, there is one other," said the beaver boy. "There is the Chinker. He has a very important job. He is the one who chinks the dam. He stops up the dam with sticks and mud, and he knows just where to put them. I help him when I flap my tail and pat out the mud on the dam."

Niklik was very interested. "I would like to see your folks," he said. "Can you take me to them?"

"Yes, surely I can. Just follow me," said the beaver boy, and away he went, swimming up the creek.

Soon he came to a big pile of sticks with mud patted down on top of them. It reached clear across the little stream. "Here is where we live," he told Niklik. "You must leave your kayak here and follow me. When I dive, you must hold your breath and dive with me."

So the orphan boy tied his kayak to a willow tree and went into the water. Down he dived with the little beaver. Soon they came to a door under the water, and the little beaver opened it into the porch of an igloo. Niklik saw many blackfish on the floor. They were all over the porch and were alive on the damp floor. They went on into the igloo. It was quite dry.

An old beaver peered at Niklik and said, "It has been a very long time since we have seen any strangers. Are you not hungry? You must have traveled very far."

It was the father beaver talking, and he said to his wife, "Bring some of our finest fish for the young man and prepare them. He is surely hungry. Bring a pike, for that is the best."

Niklik loved pike very much, and they were seldom caught at Hooper Bay. How his mouth watered as he thought of them! He was really hungry. Soon the old beaver lady came in with a dish of food.

Niklik stared in surprise. It was not pike at all but a whole bowlful of little roots that looked like mouse food. "This is not pike," the orphan boy said. "I've never eaten roots like this before. They might make me sick."

"Then bring him a Chee fish," said the father beaver. "This pike is fine, but if he has never eaten it you had better bring him a Chee fish." The mother beaver hurried out and soon returned with another bowlful of food.

Niklik looked at it. It was not Chee fish at all but another kind of root. It looked like the roots of the aspen or the willow. "This is not Chee fish," said Niklik. "I've never eaten roots like this before. I am afraid they might make me sick." He was rather embarrassed. He did not wish to offend the beavers, but he could not eat such hard, woody plants.

The father beaver seemed rather angry then. "Bring some of the old willow roots and those old leaves off the porch floor," he told his wife. "This young man is too particular. Just bring him any old thing."

The mother beaver hurried out into the porch. Soon she brought a whole dishful of blackfish. She had her nose turned up and acted as though they might soil her hands. She set them down in front of the orphan boy, and he ate them all. How good they tasted!

The beavers were quite surprised when Niklik ate the blackfish. Soon, however, they began to understand that the names they had for things were different from the names the orphan boy had for the same things.

"What an odd guest!" said the beavers to one another. "Imagine eating that old trash from the floor!"

Niklik, too, was surprised, for he had never known that beavers eat only roots and bark and vegetables. They lived in the water, so he thought that they must eat fish.

So Niklik stayed with the beavers and watched them as they made their houses and their dams. He watched the Wood Cutter as he sat down beside a tree and cut a ring around it with his sharp, chisel-like teeth. How the beavers would scamper when the tree fell down! He watched the Wood Packer carrying the logs and sticks that the Wood Cutter had cut down. Then he saw the Mud Packer bringing the mud for the dam. He watched the Chinker for hours as he carefully inspected the house and the dam and placed sticks here and dabs of mud there. The little beaver swam around a great deal and looked for enemies. Sometimes he took his strong little flat tail and patted down the mud that the Chinker had placed around so carefully.

Niklik had been gone for almost a month. One day he spoke to the father beaver. "I think I have been here long enough," he said. "You people have been very kind to me, but now I must go home."

"We were glad to have you pay us a visit," said the old beaver. "We seldom see anyone here. It is so far away. But I have a surprise for you. When you dive out of the porch of our house, walk to the top of the river-bank and then look over your left shoulder."

All the beavers bade the orphan boy good-bye, and he dived out from under the porch. He went to the top of the riverbank as the old beaver had told him to do. Then he looked over his left shoulder. He could hardly believe his eyes.

There, right before him, he saw his village, and it was only a long step home.

Chanimun

How Attu Became
a Great Hunter

MANY, many years ago, an Eskimo orphan boy named
Attu lived at Hooper Boy. Usually orphan boys have a
brother, a grandmother, or some distant relative, but
Attu had none. When he was only eight years old he
worked for the other people so that he might live and
have something to eat. In the winter he carried snow for
them to use in cooking and making tea. In the summer
he carried the water from the lake to the igloos. The
women fed him for his work. He wished to be a great
hunter and thought about this constantly.

So much did Attu think of being a great hunter that
he slept very little. Often at night he would lie awake

95

and hope that he could be a hunter and have all the seals and fish he could possibly use. He stayed in the Kashim, or Man House, because he had no home. He would listen to the tales of hunting told by the older men. In olden days, before there were schools and missions, the old men often told stories in the Kashim to teach the boys how to hunt and how to live when they grew up. The Medicine Men, too, were teachers. They told of deeds of hunting and fishing so the boys might learn how to do such things when they grew older.

When little Attu was nine, he had a new job in the village. He cleaned out the igloos and carried out the garbage for the women. But all the while he was thinking of being a great hunter. At night he would make his plans and fashion spears and bow and arrows in preparation for the day when he would be large enough to hunt. He often asked the Great Spirit to help him to be the greatest hunter in the village. By thinking about it at night, when other people were asleep, he gained great strength. So he began to be known as the boy who had faith in himself.

At ten years of age, Attu had a new job in the village. This was very hard work. He had to shovel out the porches of the igloos and keep the snow out of them. At Hooper Bay this was a very strenuous job because the snow got very deep in the wintertime. All the porches of the igloos would often be blown full of snow at night. Attu worked hard and kept thinking of the time when he would be a great hunter. He seldom slept at night, and his eyes became red from lack of sleep. He would lie awake all night and ask the Great Spirit to make him strong. So he came to believe in himself more than ever.

Often during the winter nights, little Attu would walk over to the Spring Village and spend the night there in the Kashim by himself. He would sit where he could look out of the top of the big igloo and watch the sea, thinking all the while about being a great hunter.

Years ago, all the Hooper Bay Eskimos would move to the Spring Village in the springtime. Here they would be much closer to the ocean and could hunt seals more easily. As springtime drew closer, Attu would spend all his nights alone in the Kashim of the Spring Village. Never sleeping, he would keep watch toward the sea and ask the Great Spirit for help.

Just in front of the Spring Village was a little lake. One night as Attu watched, he saw about a dozen little elves dancing and playing leapfrog along the shore. Although they saw him watching, they did not try to speak to Attu. As daylight came, they disappeared into the ground, and the orphan boy returned to the main village. He knew that to see the little elves was a very good sign, and he was sure he was getting stronger. This spring he felt certain that he would become a hunter.

The Eskimo people were preparing to move to the Spring Village. They packed their mouse food into grass baskets and tied them with strips of sealskin, just as little girls tie their hair in bowknots. Also they packed baskets with berries so that they could make Eskimo ice cream. Some baskets were filled with greens that they had found in the bottoms of the lakes. All these baskets were taken over to the Spring Village, for the Eskimos were going to move there in a few days.

That night little Attu again went to the Kashim at the Spring Village. He felt himself becoming stronger all the while as he watched from the window in the top of the big igloo. He did not sleep a wink. As he looked out into the empty village, he saw the baskets filled with mouse food, berries, and greens. Suddenly the bow-knots on top of the baskets began to move. Soon all the baskets were dancing just as the elves had danced the night before. At daylight the baskets became still again, and Attu returned to the main village.

The third night that Attu went to the Spring Village, he again watched from the window in the top of the Kashim, looking toward the sea. On a hill near the village was a graveyard. As he watched, the graves began to dance. The logs that were piled on top of the graves stood up like legs. They danced until daylight and then suddenly stopped.

Attu was not afraid, for orphan boys often see things that other people do not. He knew some very powerful medicine was coming into him. He felt strong. He asked the Great Spirit to help him more and make him a great hunter. Returning to the main village, he learned that the next day all the people would move to the Spring Village.

As darkness came the fourth night, Attu went to Spring Village. From the top of the big Kashim he looked out toward the sea. All night he watched, but he saw nothing. At daylight he went outside. Looking toward the sea again, he saw a boy of his own size coming toward him.

In his hands the boy carried great pieces of blubber. Walking straight up to Attu, he seemed about to give them to him. Instead he walked around behind him. Looking toward the sea again, Attu beheld another boy coming. He was carrying great pieces of blubber, too. The boy was larger than the first one, and older. As he drew near he, too, seemed about to give the orphan the blubber. But instead he walked around behind him.

Then came another, still larger boy carrying great pieces of blubber. Behind him came a young man carrying still more. Behind these came men who were still older, and finally the last man came. He was old and bent and his hair was gray. He, too, carried much blubber and, like those before him, acted as though he were going to give it to little Attu. Instead he passed around behind him.

Attu waited, but no more people came. Then he looked behind him. No one was there. Suddenly Attu realized what he had seen. He had been looking at his own life. The first boy was his present self. Those who followed were himself as he grew older. He knew then that he would live to be very old and would always be a great hunter.

Returning to the main village, the orphan boy packed his harpoons and his bow and arrows. Taking his kayak, he went out to the sea to hunt. The other people moved out to the Spring Village.

As soon as Attu went to hunt, he saw a large mukluk. This large seal is the finest the Eskimos can find in the Bering Sea. There are smaller seals and spotted seals, but the mukluk is the finest. The orphan boy threw his harpoon and killed the mukluk. He took it to the Spring Village, where all the people were moving into their springtime igloos. When they say the boy with the big mukluk, they were very excited.

"Look," said the old Medicine Man, "the orphan boy is now a great hunter. He has worked so hard and believed in himself so faithfully that now he is great."

Then Attu cut up his big mukluk seal and gave it all away. In Eskimo land all people give away the first seal they kill. So he divided the fine blubber with all the people. As he gave it away, he stood out in front of his igloo singing a song:

> *Come and get your blubber now;*
> *It is for you all,*
> *For the old and for the young,*
> *For the large or small.*

As Attu sang, the people came, bringing dishes to carry away the fine blubber. The orphan boy was happy. He knew he was to become a great hunter.

The next day Attu returned to the sea in his tiny kayak. Again he killed a big mukluk. This time he did not give it all away. Instead he had some fine blubber for himself, and the big mukluk skin. The skins of these big seals are the same as money to the Eskimos. It is quite a job to dress them. First the orphan boy stretched the big animal's hide upon the ground, fastening it with wooden pegs. It looked like a giant fur rug. Then he scraped all the hair off the skin and left it there to dry. It was like the covering for the end of a great drum. After the mukluk skin was as dry as paper, Attu rolled it up and put it away.

The orphan boy hunted each day and killed many mukluks. Then he dressed the skins, scraping off the hair. When the hunting season was over, he had killed so many seals that he was very rich. The pile of hair from the seals was as big as the Kashim. Everyone marveled at the great hunter he had become.

When the fishing season came, Attu took nets of braided whale sinews and set them in Hooper Bay. He would often come in with his kayak filled with salmon. He would unload it and return for another load. Seldom did he sleep when he was fishing.

So the orphan boy lived and grew old. He was the greatest hunter the village ever had. Often the old men in the Kashim would point to him and say to the boys, "You must believe in yourself to be great, even as Attu believed in himself. You must listen to the advice of the old people, work hard, and call upon the Great Spirit to make you strong."

At Hooper Bay even today the people often speak of the orphan boy who never slept but studied how to become a great hunter. Often when there is no blubber in the igloos, the women will tell the men, "If you would be more like Attu and not sleep so much, maybe you could catch plenty of mukluks, too."

It is very good for boys and girls to think hard about what they wish to do. If they work hard and ask the Great Spirit to help them, they will be great.

Chanimun

The Blubber Boy

A GREAT hunter named Netchek once lived at Hooper Bay long, long ago. He had one child, a little girl named Ooloo. She was a very pretty little girl and lived in an igloo at the end of the village with her parents. Each spring her father was the first man to fix his kayak and prepare for the hunt. Often he would bring home two mukluks at a time from the Bering Sea. When he went to the mountains to hunt, he usually got two caribou. Netchek and his family were very happy because they always had enough to eat.

When Ooloo had grown up, a young man in the village wished to marry her. They had always played together since Ooloo was quite small. He was very glad that she liked him better than she did anyone else. The mother of the young man was happy, too, because her son wished to marry the hunter's daughter. She went to see Ooloo's mother to talk about it.

Ooloo's mother listened as the young man's mother asked whether her son might marry the girl. She was pleased, for her daughter was now grown up and ready to have a home of her own.

"I am sure it will be all right," she said to the young man's mother. "However, I must ask her father. He thinks so much of our daughter that I know he will not want her to leave home." So she went to Netchek and told him that a young man wished to marry Ooloo.

Netchek sat with his head bowed, thinking deeply. He sat there for more than an hour. Ooloo peered at him nervously. She hoped very much that he would say yes.

At last he raised his eyes to the young man's mother and spoke. "I am a great hunter," he said, "and there is always much meat in our igloo. My daughter wants for nothing. I can still work for her and give her everything she needs. I do not want Ooloo to marry now."

Poor Ooloo was heartbroken. She cried and cried. The young man was very sad, too.

"If I cannot marry the boy I want," Ooloo told her mother, "I'll never marry as long as I live."

Ooloo's mother was very sorry about this, but Netchek had to be obeyed because he was the head of the family. She was sure that soon her daughter would forget her disappointment and later marry some fine hunter and have a little family of her own. But as time went on, Netchek's daughter still had not married.

Often young men in the village sent presents to Netchek. That was the way they had of asking whether they could marry Ooloo. However, she would never let her father keep the presents. She told him she would never have a husband.

"I could not have the one I wanted," she told him, "so now I want none."

Then Netchek would return the presents, and as time went on he grew quite provoked with his daughter. He knew that she needed to marry, for he was getting old and was no longer the hunter he had been.

"I think you should marry," Netchek told Ooloo one day. "Your mother and I are growing old, and soon I will have a hard time getting enough mukluks and caribou for the three of us. The next young man who asks to marry you and sends presents shall be the one you shall have."

"But I do not want to get married, Father," Ooloo wept. "I could not have the nice boy I wanted, so now I want none. I will hunt for myself when you grow old. Please do not ask me to marry now."

Then Netchek was very angry. He had been so

ashamed because his daughter had not married that long ago he had stopped going to the Man House. When he went to the Kashim the men would say, "What is the matter that Ooloo does not marry? Were you too hard a father when the nice young man asked her many years ago?"

"You'll marry the first man who sends presents," Netchek told her angrily. "If you do not, I shall marry you to . . ." he looked about the igloo, "I'll marry you to a piece of blubber."

That was a queer thing for her father to say, and Ooloo was not very worried. "How could anyone marry a piece of blubber?" she asked herself.

Having little to do, she began to make a tiny parka and boots, mittens, and clothes just like grown Eskimo people wear. She made them for a doll. Ooloo still liked to dress dolls even though she was a grown woman.

One day when Netchek awoke he found a large mukluk in front of the porch of their igloo. That meant that some young man wished to marry Ooloo and had sent a present. If Netchek took it inside the house, the young man would know that he could have the girl for his wife.

"Here is a fine mukluk," Netchek told Ooloo. "Some young man wishes to have you for his wife. I will take the mukluk into the house. You must marry him."

"I will not," Ooloo cried. "I do not wish to marry anyone. I could not have the nice young man who asked me years ago. I will not have this man or any other."

Her father was in a rage. He did not care to be disobeyed. "Then you can marry this blubber," he shouted at her. Throwing a piece of it into her lap, he went out of the house.

Poor Ooloo sobbed, and her mother tried to comfort her. "Why do you not take your ivory picture knife," she told her daughter, "and go out on the snow and make picture stories? Take this blubber with you so that you will have warm food to eat. It is very cold."

The girl went out to the end of the village to make pictures in the snow with her ivory knife. Although it was the depth of winter, the wind was not blowing, so she did not feel the cold. She thought of the blubber and took it from her pocket. It was frozen quite hard.

Sitting on the snow, Ooloo carved a little boy from the blubber. He was a fine-looking boy and reminded her of the young man whom she had wished to marry many years ago.

"What a lovely doll," she said, looking at the Blubber Boy. "I will put these doll clothes on it." So she took from her pocket the little boots and mittens and parka she had made and put them on the boy. He was very handsome. Then Ooloo stood the doll up in the snow.

"Now I will pretend that he is real," she told herself. Turning her back, she said "I wish this Blubber Boy were real so that I could marry him." She looked around at the doll again and could hardly believe her eyes. There stood a handsome young man. She had never seen him before.

She took the young man to her igloo and told Netchek, "This is to be my husband. I will marry the Blubber Boy."

How glad her father and mother were! They both liked the young man as soon as they saw him. The two were married right away and lived with Ooloo's parents.

When the first days of spring came, the Blubber Boy went hunting. Soon he had two fine mukluks and brought them home while the sun was yet high and the snow hard. Each day he went to the ocean, and always before the afternoon, when the ice and snow started to melt, he would return with mukluks, seals, and eider ducks. Netchek was very proud of his son-in-law, for he was a great hunter. Netchek would not have to hunt now.

One day, when the Blubber Boy went out, it was quite warm. He soon killed a big mukluk. Because it was so hot, he decided he would go home with it. He paddled along in his little kayak and began to feel very tired and weak and perspired a great deal. "It really is hot!" he said. "I'll be glad to get home. It is cool in the igloo."

On he paddled, and as he did he sang:

I must paddle home in my kayak,
For the sun makes me very warm.
I am tired and weak, and I'm sweating—
Am I coming to any harm?

So on he went, paddling and singing the same song. As he came near the end of the village where they lived, Ooloo heard him singing. She stopped and listened. Then she ran down to meet him as fast as she could. She knew what was wrong.

As the Blubber Boy's kayak touched the shore, Ooloo reached out and pulled it up on the bank. The young man seemed to sway forward and backward, and then he seemed to wilt as he sat there in the kayak. Ooloo ran to him. When she reached the side of the boat, she could only gasp. There on the floor of the kayak was a pile of blubber. It was soft and oily. The Blubber Boy had melted right away.

Old Netchek grumbled a lot when he found that the Blubber Boy had turned back into blubber. Now he would have to do the hunting. All the people were terribly sorry. "What a shame," they said. "Ooloo is again without a husband. He was such a nice young man."

But Ooloo was not bothered. It served her father right that he had to hunt. He had not let her marry the nice young man of her choice many years before. She sang as she made another suit of the finest doll clothes in the village. She smiled to herself as she worked. Would not winter soon be back? When it did come she could make the Blubber Boy again with her ivory picture knife. Then she could dress him in the doll clothes and wish him back to her. So Ooloo's eyes twinkled, and she sang as she made the beautiful little clothes. She knew that she did not need to worry.

Usually when a girl is determined not to marry, there is little anyone can do about it.

The Five Sisters

A GREAT many years ago, before the white people came to Alaska, there lived five sisters near Hooper Bay. Neither they nor any of the Eskimo people knew who their parents were. They did their own hunting and fishing and lived apart from the rest of the village.

They were rather peculiar girls. Four of them were not very clean. They seldom washed their hands and clothes. But the youngest sister was always spotless. Her kuspuk was washed every evening and hung by the fire to dry. She took baths regularly and kept her hair and skin nice with seal oil. Indeed, she was a fine girl.

One spring, just before the snow had melted, the five sisters went to a hill to coast. They had no sleds, but the snow was hard and they could slide down standing up, just as if they were on skis.

"Let's play a game," said the oldest. "I will go first and wish that I might be something."

Away she went, sliding down the hill. Near the bottom she tumbled head over heels, and while she lay on the snow she sang this song:

> *When I stand up, what shall I be?*
> *A plant, a bug, or fish at sea?*
> *Long I'll live and never marry—*
> *Let me be a salmonberry.*

The sister stood up and, right before the eyes of the other astonished girls, she vanished. Where she had been standing there was now a beautiful patch of salmonberries. They could hardly believe their eyes.

"Now I shall go," said the next oldest sister. Away she went, sliding down the steep hill on the hard snow. When she reached the bottom she tumbled head over heels, and before she got up she sang this song:

> *When I stand up, what shall I be?*
> *I hope that I'll be fair to see.*
> *Here I go, I must not tarry—*
> *Let me be a wild blueberry.*

The sister stood up and the rest of them gasped. Right before their eyes, she vanished. Where she had been standing there was a beautiful patch of blueberries.

"Now I shall go," cried the next oldest sister. "It will be fun to be something else." Away she went, sliding down the hill on the hard snow. When she reached the bottom she tumbled head over heels, and before she got up she sang this song:

> *When I stand up, what shall I be?*
> *Oh, watch me, sisters, then you'll see.*
> *I shall live where it's light and airy—*
> *Let me be a nice blackberry.*

The sister stood up and, before the eyes of the other two, she vanished. Where she had been standing was a beautiful patch of blackberries.

"I am going next," cried the fourth oldest sister. Away she went, sliding down the hill on the hard snow. When she reached the bottom she tumbled head over heels. Before she got up she sang this song:

> *When I stand up, what shall I be?*
> *Something that folks will want, you see.*
> *I'll be red as any cherry—*
> *Let me be a wild cranberry.*

The girl stood up and, there in front of the youngest sister, she vanished. Where she had been standing was a beautiful patch of cranberries.

Now the youngest girl, who had always been so

careful to keep herself and her clothing clean, prepared to slide down the hill. Carefully she smoothed her hair with her hands and brushed the wrinkles out of her kuspuk. Then away she went, whizzing down the hill like a bullet. When she reached the bottom she tumbled head over heels, and while she lay on the white snow she sang this song:

> *When I stand up, what shall I be?*
> *I hope I'm sweet and fair to see.*
> *Change me now, some kindly fairy—*
> *Let me be a thimbleberry.*

The nice girl stood up. At once she became the most beautiful patch of thimbleberries in the whole world. How the Eskimo people love them! They are the very finest berries in all the Far North.

And so the five sisters all became berries, to bring pleasure and cheer to the Eskimo people. That is why the little Eskimo children down near Hooper Bay often speak to the berries when they are picking them. They know that once the berries were the five sisters.

It pays to be neat and clean, for then you, too, will be as sweet as a thimbleberry and people will like you just as much.

Chanimun

The Adventures of Oolagon

Long before the white men came to Alaska, the Eskimo and Indian people had great wars. Fortunately they did not have guns in those days, or there would have been no one left in the whole country. Wars are terrible. We know that they are wrong. But when someone is trying to kill or rob you, the only thing left is to fight back.

So it was with the people at Hooper Bay. They were very poor. They lived down on the edge of the Bering Sea in their igloos made of sticks and dirt. They lived there because fierce Indian warriors had driven them into that land until, because of the ocean, they could go no farther. All they had to eat were the seals and the fish they caught. At times they went to the hills for caribou. But when they did, the Indians sometimes killed them.

Near the mouth of the Yukon lived a very warlike tribe of Indians. At times they would paint their canoes red to show that they were going to war. Then they would paddle down the rivers toward the ocean and try to kill the poor Eskimos. They would take the pokes of seal oil and blubber that the Eskimos had prepared for the hungry times in winter. Often those of the Hooper Bay people who were not killed in these raids would starve for want of food.

A little boy named Oolagon lived in the Hooper Bay village. He was very small for his age and not very strong. But he was a clever boy and was known as the boy who never made mistakes. No matter what trouble he got into, he would always think quickly and carefully and then do exactly the right thing to get out of that trouble. He was a very good hunter. He could always work out the best way to approach a seal on the ice or to get close to the emperor geese he wished to kill for food. When little Oolagon was only ten years old, the warriors from the Yukon attacked the Hooper Bay village. Many of the people were killed, but he escaped.

Oolagon's mother had had five brothers. During the wars with the Yukons, they had been killed one by one. Each had told the lad many things about the wars and how to protect himself with arrows and spear. By the time the last of the five uncles had been killed, Oolagon was a young man. He had learned much from his uncles. Although he was still quite small and not particularly strong, he was very intelligent.

One spring day, after the ice had thawed out of the rivers, Oolagon and his nephew, a lad of sixteen, went up the Kashunuk River to hunt caribou. Soon they saw one. They crept close to it and shot the beast with their arrows. The caribou was wounded and bounded away. Oolagon went in pursuit. He told the boy to wait for him until he returned. After following the caribou a great distance, the hunter went up on a little hill near the Kashunuk to try to see the animal. The minute he came to the hill, he saw about a dozen war canoes belonging to the Yukon savages in the river just below him. They were painted red. He was very close and knew that he must have been seen.

Thinking quickly, as he always did, Oolagon pretended not to see the canoes and the warriors. Instead he looked far beyond them as if he were searching for someone. Turning his back on them, he walked slowly over the hill in the direction from which he had come.

But as soon as he was out of sight, he moved swiftly. He knew that the warriors would be after him at once. He ran around the hill as fast as he could. As he ran he pulled a waterproof sealskin parka out of his little knapsack and put it on. Straight to a weedy lake he went. Jumping in so as not to leave any tracks in the mud, he crawled to a place where the grass was thick. Hastily he buried himself in the mud and moss. Only his nose stuck up above the level of the lake.

Oolagon had been none too quick. He was hardly out of sight when a dozen Yukon warriors dashed over the hill, expecting to see him very close to them. They stopped, perplexed. Could he have been a spirit? They searched everyplace. At last they went back to their canoes and on down the Kashunuk River toward the ocean. After dark, Oolagon crawled from the mossy lake and went back to where he had left his nephew. He found the lad safe and told him nothing about the warriors. He knew that the boy would be terribly frightened.

In the morning, Oolagon and the boy started back toward Hooper Bay in their kayaks. The young man kept a keen watch for the warriors. He thought they might be hiding along the river in the hope of catching him. At one place the river was very crooked, and they passed near a small stream that flowed into Hooper

Bay. The tide was low and there was no water in it. Oolagon knew that when the tide came in, they could go to Hooper Bay by that stream. He was sure that the savages did not know that this little dry stream could take them to Hooper Bay.

"Let's stop here," he suggested, "and play games." Across the crooked Kashunuk, Oolagon had seen a bunch of geese flying. They were white-fronted geese and very wily. Suddenly they flared into the sky, and the hunter knew that something at the bend in the river had scared them. He watched and next saw a red fox walk out of the willows. The fox looked behind him toward the bend in the river as if he, too, had seen something. The hunter was sure the warriors were hiding there.

"We will pretend to be spearing seals," he told the boy. "And we will not go down to the bend of the river. We will stay here by the dry creek. When it fills with the tide, we will go to Hooper Bay that way." So they laughed and played and threw their harpoons at sticks in the river. Oolagon knew that the warriors would hear them. But he was sure that they would stay hidden, expecting the boys to pass them in their kayaks when they had finished playing. Slowly the tide began running in, and the little dry stream began to fill.

"When I say the word," Oolagon told his nephew,

"we will paddle down the little stream as fast as we can. We will pretend that there is someone after us, so we will go just as swiftly and as silently as we can. We won't splash with our paddles or shout to each other." When the little stream was full of water, they did just that. Down they went as fast as they could. The terrible warriors waiting just ahead at the bend in the river did not know for a long time that they had gone. As the boys neared Hooper Bay, they shouted to the people away from their homes to hurry to the village. The Yukons were coming. At first the little nephew thought that Oolagon was joking.

At once the Hooper Bay men went to the mouth of the Kashunuk with their kayaks. They knew that they must fight for their lives. The savages would sneak into their village in the dark if they did not meet them here. Hiding under the bank, just as the Yukon warriors had hidden when they tried to catch Oolagon, the men of Hooper Bay waited. At dusk the warriors paddled past, and the Eskimos attacked. Five times Oolagon pulled back his bowstring and let an arrow fly. Each time he killed one of the warriors, and soon not one of them remained to terrify the Eskimo people.

The next night the Hooper Bay people danced in their Kashim to celebrate their victory over the Yukon warriors. Oolagon was hailed as a great hero. He not only had saved the village by warning them but had killed five of the enemy. As he danced, he twirled a short dancing wand. From it dangled five little canoes to show how many of them he had sunk. In his dancing mask he looked very fierce. Although he was still small, he was indeed a great warrior.

The Festival for the Seals

Long, long ago, the Eskimo people at Hooper Bay used to hold a festival for the seals every year. They did not actually invite the seals to dine or give them a party with Eskimo ice cream and tea. But they did hold this festival in honor of the seals, whom they liked so much. Even after the white people came to Hooper Bay, there was a festival every year. It would always bring good luck. Each spring, after the festival, the seals would come to furnish the Eskimos with food.

If there are not many seals in the spring and many people have to go hungry, to this day at Hooper Bay, people will say that they think they should hold the seal festival again.

All the Eskimo people believed that if they saved the bladder of a seal they had killed, when put back into the sea it would become another seal and return the next year. These bladders are thin little sacks that the seals have inside them; they can be blown up and look just like little white toy balloons. Whenever an Eskimo hunter killed a seal, he would hang the little balloon carefully in his igloo and save it for the seal festival.

The small boys always took a great interest in the seal festival. Some of them would be allowed to watch the men putting the seal balloons into the ocean through a hole in the ice. Then they would hear the song that the men sang as they did this.

Several days before the seal festival, the men would take all the balloons to the Man House. Long sticks would be hung up in the Man House with the balloons on them. The sticks were made to look a little like Eskimo kayaks, but to us they would have looked just like a bunch of balloons that men carry to sell at fairs and in parks. There would always be several sticks like this in the Kashim.

When the day came for the festival, all the boys in

the village would go to the Man House. At a given time, they would all run to the sticks of balloons and see who could be the first to break one of the sticks in two. There were usually more boys than sticks of balloons, so it was quite a game to see who would be the first. The boys who were lucky would be allowed to go out with the men when they put the balloons back into the water and sang their song to the seals. The rest of the boys and people of the village were not allowed to go out on the ice and watch this being done.

Before the sticks were broken, the seal balloons would move around in the Kashim and rub together, making queer little noises. People said it was because they were alive and the seals inside them were waiting to be put back into the water.

Once when there was such a festival, a little Eskimo named Natto was the first boy to break a stick. He was very glad because now he would see the little balloons being put back into the ocean. He would also hear the song the men sang. Sure enough, they all went down to the Bering Sea where a big hole had been chopped in the ice. The Medicine Man took little Natto by the hand and led him along. The little boy did not suspect what was going to happen or he would have been terribly frightened, and his mother might not have let him go. As it was, she smiled when she saw him, for she knew he had been one of the first to break the sticks in the Man House. She was very proud of her little boy.

When Natto and the men reached the ocean, carrying the seal balloons, the men began to sing:

> *Go back to the ocean, dear seals,*
> *And see all your people below,*
> *Then come back to us in the springtime*
> *When the south winds start in to blow.*

Each man would put his seal balloons into the water and push them under the ice, singing as he did so.

Suddenly the Medicine Man who was holding little Natto's arm spoke. "None of us has ever been to see the seals to find out how they are. I think it is time that someone went and told them how much we love them. I am going to go with the balloons. I am going to take little Natto with me to see that the seals get down to the big Man House in the bottom of the ocean safely."

Everyone was so surprised that he could not say a word. They all knew that sometimes the Medicine Man would go down into the sea and walk around on the bottom of the ocean. But they had never heard of anyone going to the Kashim where the seals lived.

Little Natto was so surprised that he did not have

time to think. Before he knew what had happened, the Medicine Man had pushed him through the hole in the ice, down into the cold salt water. The next thing he knew, they were walking along on the hard sand on the floor of the ocean.

They did not feel cold, and the Medicine Man talked to Natto, telling him not to be afraid, for he would get home safe and sound to his mother and father. The seal balloons were swimming along through the water all around them. They made queer little noises, as if the seals were singing, happy to be going home again.

After the man and the boy had traveled very far down into the ocean, the water became darker. It was hard to see. The Medicine Man told Natto that this was because the water was so deep that the light from the outside world could not get down there. Suddenly they saw what looked like a large hill in front of them. As they drew closer, they saw that it was a great Man House.

In front of the door was a large fat old walrus with long whiskers and tusks. He spoke to little Natto and to the Medicine Man. "We are glad you came to pay us a visit, Medicine Man. The little boy is very welcome, too. You may stay here as long as you wish, and then you may go back to your people."

The walrus opened the door, and in walked the

Medicine Man and little Natto. All the funny little seal balloons came in, too. The moment they got inside they began to get bigger and bigger. Then suddenly each one burst with a "pop" and in its place was a seal.

Natto had never seen anything like this in his life. Some of the balloons turned into spotted seals and some into little hair seals. Others became very large mukluk seals, and Natto saw a few that turned into white baby seals with smooth, pretty fur.

"How nice it is," Natto told the Medicine Man, "that the little seals can come back to life. I will not feel so bad now when I eat one."

"It is very nice," the Medicine Man answered. "That is why we do not feel sad when we have to catch a seal for food. Come, let us walk about and see all the sea animals down here."

Little Natto took the Medicine Man's hand, and they started walking through the big Kashim. The seals did not seem to notice them. Natto wondered whether they were like ghosts so that the seals could not see them. In one place he saw ten white baby seals. They were playing with a large red ball. One would balance it on his nose and then throw it to his neighbor. That little seal would have to catch it on his nose and pass it to the next, and so on. If a little seal dropped the ball, he would have to get out of the game, and the rest would play on. Finally a teeny-weeny seal and a much larger one were the only ones left in the game. They threw the ball back and forth so fast that little Natto could hardly see it. Suddenly the biggest seal dropped the ball, so the tiny seal won the game. Then all the other little seals made a funny little grunting cough, which was their way of laughing. They clapped their funny little flippers together in glee.

At another place in the Kashim, little Natto saw several big old papa walruses. They were all fast asleep and snoring very loud. Sometimes tiny baby walruses would crawl up on their big backs and go sliding down, just as if they were coasting on sleds down a hill. The big walruses didn't even wake up.

"Now," said the Medicine Man, "we will see the biggest animals in the world. They stay down here at one end of the Kashim." He went far down to the end of the giant room, which was larger than a circus tent. There little Natto saw the whales, the biggest animals in the world. Some of them were so large that it took him several minutes to walk around them. Most of them were sleeping. Some had their eyes open and looked very friendly.

Natto saw little white whales like those that came into the shallow water at Hooper Bay. He also saw huge bowhead whales. He thought that there could be nothing in the world as big as these. One old whale was especially big. He was so old that his skin looked like the side of a ship with seaweed and moss on it. In his back there were several harpoons where men had shot him. He was so old and tough that they did not hurt him at all.

"What are those sleek, pretty little animals over there?" Natto asked the Medicine Man. "I've never seen any of those at Hooper Bay."

"Those are the sea otters," the Medicine Man replied. "There are not many of them left in the world. People killed so many of them for their beautiful skins that there are hardly any left to swim about in the sea."

"They are very beautiful," said little Natto. "But they do look sad. Why don't people send their balloons back so they can live again, as we do with the seals?"

"I guess that the people do not know how to do that where the sea otters live," replied the Medicine Man. "But come now, let us see if there are any other sea animals you would like to see."

"Oh, what is that funny thing?" little Natto asked excitedly. "It looks like a great big Eskimo bowl with short legs on it."

The Medicine Man laughed. "Why, that is a giant sea turtle. He is very old, even older than the whales. Some of the animals here say he is almost a thousand years old. He is very wise and often the animals ask him questions. He can remember back almost to the first thing that happened in the world."

So little Natto and the Medicine Man walked about in the giant Man House admiring all the animals. The Man House was so large that they walked for many hours and saw only a small part of it.

After a long time, little Natto said, "I am very thirsty. Where can we get a drink of water?"

"All of the water here is salty," the Medicine Man told him. "I will have to make magic to get you fresh water. All of these animals can live on seawater. But I know you cannot." Then the Medicine Man took a wand that he carried and began to bore a hole in the soft sand of the floor of the Man House. As he did so, he sang a funny little song.

"You must take the biggest swallows you can," advised the Medicine Man, "for you will get only five swallows of water. After you take five swallows, the water will stop and I will have to make my magic all over again." The Medicine Man went on singing, and suddenly out of his wand there came a stream of clear, cold, sweet water.

Little Natto leaned over the water. It was just like a drinking fountain. Carefully he took the longest, biggest swallows he could. One—two—three—four—five.

Then the water stopped, as abruptly as it had begun. "I feel much better," sighed Natto, "but I would really like to have more. When may I drink again?"

"Twice every day you may have water," the Medicine Man told him. "That will be enough for you, I know. Come now, we must see more of the animals and learn more about them. I want to ask them if they are all satisfied and if there is anything we can do for them."

After a while, little Natto and the Medicine Man came before the largest seal they had ever seen. He was bigger than two kayaks. "This is the King of the Seals," said the Medicine Man. "Let us talk with him. . . . O King of the Seals," said the Medicine Man, "we are from the earth above and wish to talk with you. Will you tell us if there is anything we should do for the seals when they come to our shores?"

The large old seal looked very wise and blinked his sleepy eyes. "No, Mr. Medicine Man," he replied, "I think all the Eskimo people are very careful of the seals. As long as they will always take good care of the little seal balloons and send them safely home every year, we will be happy. We want to help the Eskimos. Our people will always come to your shores, just as long as you are good to us."

So little Natto and the Medicine Man thanked the

old seal and went on in the big Kashim. "How long have we been away?" little Natto asked. "When will we be going home again? It is so strange down here. I feel as if I have been here no more than a day, but it seems a long time since I saw my mother and father. And I am thirsty, too. May I have another drink?"

The Medicine Man bored a hole in the floor and again said the magic words. Out came the fresh water. One—two—three—four—five. Little Natto swallowed five big swallows.

"We will start back now," said the Medicine Man. Going to the door of the big Man House, he knocked three times.

The large old walrus with the long whiskers opened it. "Come back again, little Natto and Mr. Medicine Man," he said. "I hope you have a nice journey as you walk back on the bottom of the sea to your homes."

"Thank you, Mr. Walrus," said little Natto and the Medicine Man. And off they started.

"How do we know which way to go?" little Natto asked the Medicine Man. "I hope we do not get lost and that I will get home in time for supper."

The Medicine Man smiled to himself and then answered, "We will not lose our way, for I am a Medicine Man. My wand will lead me straight home." And sure enough, the wand in the Medicine Man's hand seemed to be pulling them in one direction.

As they walked on and on, it appeared to be growing lighter. Little Natto remarked about this to his companion.

"Yes," said the Medicine Man, "the water is getting shallower. We are getting nearer to the land. Soon we will be home again. Just wait and see."

"How will we get up through the ice again?" Little Natto looked worried. "Maybe the hole where we put the balloons will be frozen over."

"I would not worry about that," the Medicine Man replied quietly with a smile. "But look how light it is now. We must be almost there."

Suddenly, as they walked, the Medicine Man's head appeared to be missing. It frightened little Natto terribly until a few seconds later, when his own head came up out of the water. Then he saw the Medicine Man smiling at him. They had walked right up out of the ocean, and in front of them was the village of Hooper Bay.

"Why, where is all the ice and all the snow?" Little Natto was so surprised that he could hardly talk. "Look, the hills are green, and I can see salmonberries on the tundra."

"It is summertime, little Natto," the Medicine Man said. "We have been gone almost a year. But come, we must see all the people. They will be very surprised to see us."

Little Natto's mother hugged him hard when she saw him. Everyone crowded around to see them and touch them. No one had ever been to the Kashim of the seals or spent a year beneath the ocean before. They talked far into the night, telling all the Eskimo people what they had seen and how they had talked to the King of the Seals.

"We must always treat the seals kindly," the Medicine Man said, "and we must hold a festival for them every year and send them home again."

Little Natto drank as much fresh, sweet water as he wished. He could have as many swallows as he wanted. His mother gave him a large bowlful of salmonberries, too.

"It *is* nice to be home again," he told his mother. "I think this is the best place in the world." She agreed with him.

It is always good to get home again after being gone a very long time.